# Hotel du Pont Story

# Hotel

# du Pont Story

WILMINGTON, DELAWARE

1911 - 1981

## Harry V. Ayres

SERENDIPITY PRESS

SECOND PRINTING, AUGUST, 1982
THIRD PRINTING, FEBRUARY, 1983
FOURTH PRINTING, APRIL, 1984
FIFTH PRINTING, AUGUST 1984

Hotel du Pont Story

Copyright © 1981 E. I. du Pont de Nemours & Co.
Published by Serendipity Press, Building C, Suite 102,
3801 Kennett Pike, Wilmington, Delaware 19807

Library of Congress catalog card number 81-84301

ISBN 0-914988-07-7

Printed in the United States of America

Design by Frank Coburn

# Contents

Chapter Five • *Behind the Scene*

Chapter Six • *Unusual Roles*

Chapter Seven • *Crossroads*

*Appendices*

# Preface

*A classic of old tradition,*
*A hallmark of hospitality.*

The Hotel du Pont was built and is owned and operated by E. I. du Pont de Nemours & Co. (Inc.). This ownership was unique in the American free enterprise system in 1911, and indeed it still is today.

Its location within the corporate office complex of the Du Pont Company makes the Hotel the "front door" for business in Wilmington and most of Delaware. The Hotel in its illustrious career has hosted presidents, nobility, statesmen, industrialists, scientists, socialites, dignitaries, performing artists, sports figures, and business leaders from around the world. We have not attempted to invade the privacy of any of these guests. This story is an effort to put into place the records of all available material touching upon the history and growth of the Hotel, to recapture the spirit of its early years, and discuss many of the events and accomplishments that give it character.

A viable operation for sixty-eight years, the Hotel du Pont has been able to survive wars, depressions, increased taxes, and changes in social evaluation. Because of its total involvement in its reason for being, the guest, there have been many rewards as well as disappointments. It has been rich in providing services that dignify all plateaus of society.

The investment at the time of construction was more than twice the usual one for a first class hotel of its size. Today, it is a relatively modest investment for the Du Pont Company. There is agreement that the Hotel du Pont is a picture window through which the public may look at the character of the company. It plays an important role in the area of public relations. It is a hotel of quiet elegance, homelike and attractive in the highest degree.

# Acknowledgments

I appreciate the confidence and approval given to me when I started this project by James C. Stewart, retired director of the General Services Department of the Du Pont Company, the support and approval for publication by Don L. Longenecker, present director of the General Services Department, and the follow-up, arrangements, and excellent cooperation by Ferdinand Wieland, present general manager of the Hotel du Pont. I would like to thank an old friend and author, C. A. Weslager, for his counsel; Domenico Mortellito, for giving his time to en courage and advise me in the fields of art and architecture; Dora Kaufman, so helpful with information outlining the history of The Studio Group, Inc.; James A. Grady, retired director of the General Services Department, for his recollections over twenty years; Stanley L. Williams, for his help and cooperation in the field of safety; William F. Doerflinger, Playhouse manager, for his assistance; Granville Smith, for his early memories of the Hotel du Pont and the excellent information he provided; Clarence A. Bader, for his knowledge of early construction by his family's firm; Casper Fennel, for his computerized memory covering many years; John Palmer, for his well-kept diaries; Francis Rogers, for his interest and excellent information; the staff of the Eleutherian Mills Historical Library, Greenville, for information from the Pierre S. du Pont and John J. Raskob papers; the News-Journal Co., for the use of their files; the Hotel du Pont, for access to its accumulation of information and photographs over the years; and the many pensioners and members of the present staff of the Hotel, for their outstanding support and wonderful anecdotes.

My thanks also go to J. Blan van Urk, president, and Frederick H. Pollard, vice president, of Serendipity Press. Mr. Pollard was constructive and helpful throughout the publication process.

There are two persons to whom I owe a very special debt of appreciation: Carolyn F. Grubb, for her enthusiasm, dedication to the project, excellent input, and typing and retyping the large amount of material; Mrs. Grubb had been employed by the Hotel du Pont for ten years, and for her to return and be a meaningful part of this story is special indeed. And Ann Morris Aydelotte, the editor, for her sharp pencil, patience, expertise, and ability to make me feel comfortable as changes were made; she has shown professionalism at its finest.

Finally, to my family and friends, too numerous to mention, thank you.

HARRY V. AYRES

*Wilmington*
*1981*

PERSONS
TRESPASSING
on the GRASS
will be
PROSECUTED

*The location of the Hotel before construction started*

*The architect's drawing of the proposed Hotel du Pont submitted for approval in 1911*

The First Decade

# How It Came About

At the turn of the century, Wilmington was expanding and becoming a city of corporate headquarters. Demands for hotel accommodations were increasing. A new hotel of any magnitude had not been built in Wilmington since the Clayton House in 1873. Visitors coming to town to conduct business and finding it necessary to stay overnight were hardpressed to obtain accommodations. Some were invited to stay at the homes of company officials; however, this arrangement was not always convenient or desirable. Other visitors had to travel to Philadelphia for lodgings.

Hotel promoters, aware of this need, had been calling on Pierre S. du Pont and John J. Raskob to discuss the possibility of a joint venture for a new hotel in Wilmington. While Mr. du Pont, a sure, precise, and shy administrator, and Mr. Raskob were not men with any hotel background, both were deeply concerned for the Du Pont Company and for the needs of the community. After a number of discussions, Mr. du Pont wrote a letter to the Office Buildings Division of the company on May 3, 1911. "The thought occurred to us that if a hotel in Wilmington was as good a proposition as he [the promoter] was inclined to believe, it might be well worth considering in con-

1

nection with our building," that is, with the proposed third section of the Du Pont Building to be erected at 11th and Market Streets. Following this letter, a meeting for further discussion was arranged by Mr. du Pont with Mr. Raskob, whose motto was "Go Ahead and Do Things," R. R. M. Carpenter, an internationally known sportsman and brother-in-law of Pierre, and T. Coleman du Pont; all four were or would be key executives of E. I. du Pont de Nemours & Co. (Inc.). The only person with some background in hotel administration was Coleman, the president of the Du Pont Company and a man of energy and vision, although his field was primarily in investment in hotels. In fact, by 1920 Coleman would control with L. M. Boomer & Associates several New York hotels, including the McAlpin and the Waldorf-Astoria, as well as the Bellevue-Stratford in Philadelphia and the Willard in Washington.

Should we have been able to listen in on their discussions, we might have heard: Is a new hotel really needed? If so, what are the alternatives? Should a manufacturing company plunge into such a difficult and unrelated business? What will it cost? Will it be profitable? What about location? Size? Number of rooms and support facilities? Who will manage it? What about the staff? The architecture? Are workmen available to implement these plans? We can imagine the frustration and doubt experienced by the group on these and many other concerns.

After a moment of quiet and reflection, Pierre S. du Pont said, "Well, gentlemen, what is your recommendation?" A voice thought to be that of Mr. Raskob said, with a lot of feeling and in a very positive manner, "Let's build it!" The meeting's tempo changed; there was enthusiasm! Approval to proceed with plans was obtained.

A second meeting was arranged for the purpose of deciding on the character of the new hotel. The deep concern for the Du Pont Company's and community's needs was in place. To serve these needs required more than just a building to accommodate visitors; it must be a master achievement in hotel architecture and ingenuity. It must be of the highest quality, without compromise, elegant yet homelike, and attractive to the greatest degree. It must contain every facility for the entertainment and comfort of the people of Wilmington and the travelling public for years to come. The Hotel du Pont must give the city of Wilmington the distinction of having one of the most beautiful and best appointed hostelries in the country.

The Hotel must serve the individual first and the community next, as an integral part of both, as the heartbeat of the community. It must be a cornerstone in service. It must give the best because the best is required; the taste of the Hotel must be that of its patrons. It must not venture into the privacy of its guests nor invite intrusions. And all this must recreate the atmosphere of a most comfortable home.

The first modern hotel man, Ellsworth M. Statler, said, "The first and most important consideration when you decide to erect a hotel is location." The Hotel du Pont would be located in the heart of Wilmington at the corner of 11th and Market Streets, on a hill overlooking the historic Brandywine, Christina, and Delaware rivers and the proposed new civic square. The Hotel could hardly be situated to better advantage, at the hub of the city. Placed at the upper end of the business and professional sections and at the beginning of the residential section, it would draw all avenues of civic life to it. The largest commercial houses, theaters, clubs, and public buildings were in the immediate vicinity; it was close to a major highway, Route 13, and within ten minutes of two busy railroad stations.

The plans called for a hotel with 150 bedrooms, supplemented by a main dining room, rathskeller, men's café and bar, ballroom, club room, ladies' sitting room, and appropriate kitchen and housekeeping facilities. No expense was to be spared. This was an ambitious undertaking for a city with a population of 80,000.

The question of who would operate the Hotel was raised during the early planning meetings. The Du Pont Company itself lacked such expertise. T. Coleman du Pont answered, "We will employ the experts we need from other well-known properties." Ernest S. Taite, manager of the Astor Hotel in New York, was hired as the first manager of the Hotel du Pont and reported for duty, as construction started, to Pierre S. du Pont, president of the specially created Hotel Du Pont Co. This company would have administrative responsibility for the Hotel and monitor operating procedures.

As construction moved forward, department heads were selected to operate the property. Four were former employees of the Astor. The executive chef came from the Gotham Hotel in New York and brought with him twenty food preparation experts. The departmental staff was completed with eight other key employees from hotels in other cities. The only local person to be employed as a department head during this period came from the Clayton House in Wilmington. It was the custom in those days for each department head to bring his team for the opening. This group would have the responsibility for selecting and training employees from the Wilmington area. The training would not be an easy task for these department heads, nor would it be easy for the new employees.

With the opening approaching, everyone worked hard to be ready to perform professionally. In November 1912, a meeting was called to discuss communications among the various departments so that the heads might get to know one another. Each made a brief progress report, since the day for the opening was set for January 15, 1913. This date had special significance, since it was Pierre S. du Pont's birthday. The executive chef, E. Garraux, reported that he had met with the maitre d'hôtel to discuss menus. The items would be of the highest quality, beautiful and simple. In fact, the preparations would establish a standard for years to come. Of course, he said, the food must be served with great expertness; "I hope the service will not break down." To these remarks, the maitre d'hôtel, with all the sharpness he could muster, said, "Chef, please prepare the food." The wine steward, J. E. C. Donnelly, reported that all

# Hotel du Pont

## Wilmington, Del.

---

## Opening

## January 15th 1913

*First Lobby, 1913*

*Reception Room*

the wines required were available. James J. Nolan, the chief steward, stated that all the china, glass, and silver had arrived. Margaret T. MacManus, executive housekeeper, reported that all linen had arrived and was washed and ready for use. The sterling silver brushes, mirrors, and combs had been received for the bedrooms. John A. Akehurst, the chief valet, reported that all uniforms had been received. The uniformed personnel were now reporting for issue and fitting; each employee would be flawless in dress. Maintenance men were busy with uncompleted details and follow-up on all items not yet in hand. All seemed to be going well for the big day. Everyone realized the clock was running.

On December 15, 1912, a meeting was called to assign detailed responsibilities. During this meeting, the tempo and excitement increased. Now for important details: the guest list, parking, transportation, police for traffic and crowd control, internal security, rooms for the press and prominent Delawareans, the location for a doctor, arrangements for music, decorations, flowers for the tables, gifts for the ladies, guides to conduct tours, arrangements for guests needing special help, area coverage, and the establishment of an information center. The final words every employee heard from the manager were, "Follow up, assume nothing, check again and again." To assist Mr. Taite, Sarah H. Truax was hired in early January as his executive secretary, a position she would fill capably for forty years for five of the seven managers.

On January 10, 1913, a final review was necessary before the opening five days later. Confirmed reservations for the Main Dining Room and Grille totaled 295 guests, primarily from Delaware and nearby states. Due to so many requests for the opening night, these dinners would be repeated on the following night.

Many people phoning did not believe the Hotel was filled. Some of those who called wanted to know if the opening was just for society folks, and did you have to know someone to get a reservation? One lady with a beautiful voice said, "Now don't tell me you cannot find one more seat, particularly for me." The switchboard was swamped for the last few days before the opening. There was simply no more space.

Although the doors were not open officially, more than fifty persons were registered and already occupying rooms. Wesley Webb of Dover, a member of the State Horticultural Society, was the first to register. He and other members of the society were to attend the Corn Show to be held in the ballroom. The employees chuckled at this announcement; what they were planning would not be a "corn" show. Mr. Raskob was the first to engage a suite of rooms. He and his wife planned to reside at the Hotel during the winter. Pierre S. du Pont, then a bachelor, had discussed the location of the number of rooms he would require for a suite. Twenty other inquiries had been made concerning suites to be used by permanent guests.

The morning newspaper on January 13 announced that the Hotel du Pont would open on January 15. The wait finally was over. Few occasions caused so much excitement for the city, indeed for the entire state. Delawareans, whose curiosity and interest were now intense, would make their own appraisal of their new hotel.

# Grand Opening and Tour

Let us now relive the opening. The weather on the morning of January 15, 1913, is nice, the temperature at forty degrees. The inaugural ceremonies are to be conducted by the Sons of Delaware.[1] The electric trolleys are filled, all five taxi cabs are busy, and the roads leading to the Hotel are crowded with carriages and with the sputtering sounds of Stanley Steamers, Pierce Arrows, and other grand automobiles of the period. The streets around the Hotel are barricaded by the police to control the crowds. Downstate Delawareans are arriving in groups. Some will tour and have lunch in the dining room, and others will stay for the gala evening.

At 8 a.m., the Men's Café and Bar is crowded. Lines of expectant visitors are forming. It is all the police can do to maintain order. The crush does not ease at all during the day and evening; everyone in the city wants to see the new hotel.

The first group to be conducted on a tour, fourteen Du Pont

[1] The Sons of Delaware was an organization of Delawareans who lived in Pennsylvania and Maryland and returned to their native state to discuss programs and developments taking place in Delaware. Leadership was provided by D. H. Grier. Meetings took place in the Hotel, and the organization was discontinued in 1940. Information was furnished by W. Emerson Wilson, a noted Delaware historian and writer for the News-Journal Co. (Wilmington).

corporate executives, is led by Mr. Taite, assisted by Pierre S. du Pont and Mr. Raskob, president and secretary-treasurer of the Hotel Du Pont Co. The tour has hardly started when questions are asked, "What is the square footage, how much did it cost to build per square foot, how does that compare to other hotels, will the employees be on the company's payroll, how much return on the investment and when?" The manager is not prepared for such questions. Mr. du Pont answers them quietly and articulately.[2] After the tour, the group agrees the Hotel is beautiful architecturally; it will be an asset to the company and to the community at large. Public relations are discussed in detail. Little does Mr. Taite realize how much Du Pont Company management would be involved in future decisions. The Hotel Du Pont Co. is in operation.

The second tour, for the press and invited guests from the state judiciary, legislators, representatives from all branches of government, and politicians of importance, is invited to make an inspection of the facilities at 10 a.m. The comments and questions of this group differ from those of the corporate executives. The construction of such a hotel by the Du Pont Company clearly demonstrates the firm's interest and confidence in the community. The Hotel will be important in attracting business enterprises and in functioning as a civic center; employment possibilities in the city will improve; purchasing power will be helpful to companies providing supplies and services. Wilmington will take pride in its beautiful architecture. A few of those on the tour are heard to say, "A real tax plum." The press is astonished at the magnitude of the project. Following this tour, luncheon is served with no attempt at speechmaking.

All through the afternoon, a steady stream of people passes through the Lobby. Now the tour guides, highly excited, begin

[2] Sixty-three years later, such questions were to be raised by the president of the Du Pont Company during the planning for the Green Room Lounge when he asked, "Isn't the square foot cost of property located at 11th and Market Streets rather expensive to be used for such a project?" This area of concern was the same then and is today.

conducting tours of the Hotel for groups of twenty-five at a time. Little do the guides realize that during the week 25,000 visitors will tour the Hotel facilities. They open their remarks by reminding the visitors of the statements by the founders who had put it all in place: "Nothing would be spared to erect a hotel costing over a million dollars." Let us go along with one of the groups on the tour.

### EXTERIOR CONSTRUCTION[3]

The exterior of the building is an excellent adaptation of the Italian Renaissance period, made to conform to the modern style of tall building construction. Built entirely of white stone, the Market Street side is plain in design while on the 11th Street side, the main entrance to the Hotel, the structure is relieved by decorative window balconies placed at eye-pleasing intervals. On this side, a heavy stone coping and balcony define the first floor of the building and, as a crowning feature to the design, a handsome balustrade of stone finishes the top. On arrival, we see two flags floating over the marquee, one the national flag, the other the Hotel Du Pont Co. flag.

### RECEPTION ROOM

As we come in the main entrance, we pass beneath the handsome iron and opal glass marquee and find ourselves in the Reception Room, the whole a beautiful work of art. The floors are mosaic and terrazzo,[4] classic and cool in the summer,

[3] Information describing the property is taken largely from the booklet, *Hotel Du Pont* (Wilmington: 1920), prepared by the Hotel under the direction of Ernest S. Taite, its first manager.

[4] The reader might like to know about the materials mentioned in this chapter. *Mosaic* floors were made by inlaying colored marble chips in intricate designs; the chips had been brought in bags from Italy. *Terrazzo* floors were mosaics made by embedding marble or granite in mortar, which then was polished. *Scagliola* was an imitation marble composed of a substratum of finely ground gypsum mixed with glue, surfaced with marble dust, and polished; it was often used for columns. *Parquet* floors were of wood inlaid in different grains and colors to create a geometric pattern; workmen called them talking floors as they aged, because they made various sounds when walked upon. *Roseal* marble was hard marble imported from Italy and rose in color. *Travertine* was an Italian stone of volcanic origin formed by deposits from springs or stream waters.

now covered with luxurious Baluchistan rugs in warm colors. As we look around, we see embroidered valances with filet laces hung in the windows, which cast a soft and restful light upon the marble walls and mosaic floors. Stately woodburning fireplaces, built of Caen stone in natural colorings, occupy sites on either side of the room. Above the mantels are ornamental crests bearing the name du Pont, carved on great stone blocks. The mahogany furniture, Colonial in design, gives to the room an atmosphere of refinement and good living.

LOBBY

From the Reception Room, an approach of several marble steps and a spacious marble walled and mosaic floored aisle leads to the Lobby. We stand in awe at its magnificence. Designed in rather severely plain Italian Renaissance style, with wainscoting of softly tinted Italian marble and supporting scagliola pillars of dark colorings, this area shows a delightful contrast in soft grays. Above, the walls and ceiling are of Caen stone, while in the center of the ceiling is an exquisite piece of leaded multicolored glass through which the daylight penetrating casts a pleasing, soft light over the Lobby. From the center of the skylight hangs a stately electrolier of finished brass with light subdued by tinted shades. The frosted bell-shaped globes, ornamented with light blue, are unusually effective.

The care given to both the architecture and decoration of the Lobby makes it cheerful as well as charming. A fine painting by the late Howard Pyle, his last work, hangs over a massive fireplace. It depicts a Du Pont prairie schooner, or covered wagon, hauling black powder from the Brandywine mills during the War of 1812. Large comfortable davenports, deep upholstered armchairs, and gorgeous Baluchistan rugs upon the marble floors provide ease and comfort for guests. The marble registration desk is located on the west side of the Lobby.

*Main Dining Room*

*Grille Room*

*Rose Room*

*Men's Café and Bar*

### ROSE ROOM

The main salon is an entrancing reproduction of the Louis XIV period, of warm French gray stucco work relieved with old ivory. The draperies at the doors and windows are a rich tone of red brocaded velvet, with handsome filet laces in the casements. A large Louis XIV mirror enhances the effect, which is completed by a beautiful inlaid hardwood floor. The carpets were woven expressly for this room. We cannot imagine a more correct or lovely reproduction of the period it represents. Elegant and attractive, it is intended as a ladies' sitting room, but occasionally lectures and dinner parties will be held here.

### MAIN DINING ROOM

From the Lobby, we enter this great room. The dining room is lit by inverted domes which bathe the ceiling and room in a soft, comfortable glow. We are amazed at the high ceiling which rises two and a half stories, decorated in colors of old ivory with brown and forest green, finished in gold. The walls of quartered oak panelling complement the large oak ceiling beams. As we glance above to the right, we see a musicians' gallery overlooking the room. The windows are decorated with tapestry of the same shade of forest green. Furnishings are oak to harmonize with the panelling. The elegant marble floor is a delicate mosaic covered with Oriental rugs of rich design. This room is stately and formal to the highest degree.

### MEN'S CAFÉ AND BAR

Conveniently located on the ground floor and accessible from the Lobby, the Men's Café opens onto Market Street. We at once admire its simplicity and beauty. The room is treated with a heavy beamed ceiling, harmonizing with the high wainscoting and columns of fumed chestnut. Above the wainscoting are a number of marine scenes executed by one of Wilmington's young artists, Charles de Feo. Furniture, in Mission style, matches the woodwork and is very pleasing.

## PEACOCK ALLEY

We now walk through a large hallway between the Lobby and the Club Room. It is handsomely panelled in imported walnut, with writing desks along the wall. The flooring is parquet covered with a beautifully designed runner. In this hallway, guests will write letters and watch other guests promenade in their finery. To the right is a stock brokerage firm, a billiards room, the telephone exchange, and executive offices. We move down the hallway to enter the Club Room.

## CLUB ROOM

The Club Room, to be used primarily as a sitting room or for lectures and private dinner parties, is panelled entirely with Italian walnut, beautifully handcarved. Around the top of the panelling is a decorative motif set with beavers and pelicans and a wheel, to portray the Protestant work ethic of keeping one's shoulder to the wheel. As we admire the panelling, we notice a door that appears to go nowhere. In October, it will open into the lobby of the newly completed Playhouse, so that playgoers may mingle and have beverages at intermission in the European custom.

A handsome batik, *A Legend of Hospitality,* hangs over the fireplace. This batik, dyed in thirteen colors on silk for the Hotel by the painter, Arthur Crisp, measures eleven by fourteen feet and is one of the most ambitious works of its kind ever attempted.

We look up to see three circular skylights of leaded glass, in marine motifs. The first depicts a ship of Lord De La Warr's period; the second, a frigate during the War of 1812 when Wilmington was gaining renown as a shipbuilding community; and the third, a modern destroyer. We look down to see a beautifully polished parquet floor and carpeting.

### GRILLE

As we enter the Grille, on the lower level, its architecture reflects charm and informality. At the entrance is a huge fireplace where a roaring fire is lit. The floor is of large red tiles. The low ceilings and quaint lights throw a soft, warm glow over the entire room and outline the heavy oak furnishings and quietly lit booths around the walls. The high wainscoting and supporting pillars, topped with little grotesque gnomes, are of fumed oak beautifully carved in Gothic designs. A small comfortable bar located on the right is in keeping with the rathskeller atmosphere. The bandstand is located in the center of the room, and musicians who will live in the Hotel will provide dance music nightly.

### MEZZANINE

Above the Lobby is the mezzanine floor, or delightful Palm Court, with a handsomely wrought balustrade of iron and brass. It is finished in the same style as the Lobby and is on a line with the beautiful mirrored windows placed high in the walls of the Lobby. Decorative balconies, filled with tropical plants, are placed beneath these windows. It is one of the most inviting areas of the Hotel. The furniture is of the Elizabethan period, contrasting with marble walls and white Caen stone columns. Teas and other entertainments, including dancing, will be enjoyed by young people who will stop in for an hour's diversion. Concerts are to be given daily by the Hotel orchestra. Private dining rooms, which seat from five to fifty guests, are located on the Market Street side; these rooms are finished in Circassian walnut, with soft gray tapestry walls and hangings in old gold and crimson.

From the Mezzanine we can look down on the Lobby and see why many refer to it as a "marble palace." We move a little farther, looking out over the Rose Room, and find ourselves wanting to touch the great ceiling of the room.

## BALLROOM

We now take the elevator to the eleventh floor, the lobby of the Ballroom. This room, placed in operation before the Hotel officially opened, is elegant in every aspect of fine architecture. The arched ceiling and beautiful panelled walls are finished in old ivory with touches of bright gold. The magnificently finished dance floor is much admired by all followers of the terpsichorean art. The room is fitted with a stage and adjoining rooms and all the accouterments for light theatricals, seating 500 persons. A handsomely appointed ladies' retiring room and six private dining rooms are located nearby on the same floor.

## BEDROOMS

After seeing the public rooms, we now visit the guest floors. The corridors are wide and of marble. Thick Axminster carpets ensure absolute quiet. No new developments or innovations have been spared to provide the most up to date guest rooms in the world. The 150 rooms are divided into three classes: suites, double rooms, and single rooms, and communicating rooms are available. The suites have sitting rooms attractively decorated and furnished in period style, each with a large fireplace adding a distinct air of hominess. Hardwood floors are covered with thick, soft rugs; while the furnishings are luxurious, comfort has not been sacrificed for beauty. A boudoir, with dressing table and every toilet convenience, and a private bath are provided with each bedroom. The beds are of polished brass and are made up with imported linen. On each dresser is a sterling silver comb, brush, and mirror, pin cushion with needle and thread, thimble, and buttons for quick repairs. A small highly polished brass cuspidor is placed in each room.

The bedrooms have every modern convenience. In the bathrooms, the bathtubs are of the rapidly filling and emptying type. Circulating filtered ice water is connected in each room together with a telephone and mail indicator, a small electric illuminated

*Peacock Alley, 1913*

*Club Room, 1913*

*Sitting Room, Bedroom and Bath*

*The first Ballroom, 1912*

device upon the wall which automatically reports the placing of mail in the guest's box in the office. Another innovation is the maid's announciator, whereby the switchboard operator instantly can locate and telephone the nearest maid for guest service; the maid carries a key to insert in a socket outside each room, which causes a lamp to light on the annunciator board.

Electric fans and specially devised ventilators maintain comfort in each room. During warm weather, the temperature is cooled from ten to fifteen degrees by the air cooling system installed in conjunction with the Hotel's own ice manufacturing plant. Nothing has been spared for total guest comfort.

### HOUSEKEEPING DEPARTMENT

The laundry and maids' living quarters are located on the twelfth floor, while the valet shop and housemen's facilities are on the eleventh floor. The laundry capacity is that for a 300-room hotel; it is complete in every respect and capable of taking care of the needs of a sizeable town. The valet shop and laundry are supervised by the executive housekeeper and professional valet.

### KITCHEN

Seemingly unlimited space is provided for this production area. The equipment includes every modern laborsaving device. The service stations such as storage-refrigeration, cleaning area for soiled dishes, controls for rapid and accurate service, china, glass, and silver room, cooking ranges and heaters for keeping china and food warm, are all professionally arranged for efficient production. The chefs are highly specialized in each branch of culinary art. The bake shop is staffed with the finest pastry cooks available. A combination of gas and coal (primarily coal) is used for cooking. The cold storage plant and ice machinery are most important for the refrigeration system.

The silverware, 8,000 pieces, is worth over $10,000 and

weighs more than one and a half tons. Of the finest hotel quality, it is a plain pattern with beaded and reed decorations made by Gorham and butler and polish finished. All the silverware is marked with the name Hotel du Pont.[5]

The china and glass are beautifully designed. The china is ivory with a gold band and is distinguished by the Hotel crest. The glassware is also crested. The combination of carefully designed china, glass, silver, and linen complements the dining room and creates an atmosphere of elegance.

The tour is now complete. As we leave the Lobby, we leave the atmosphere of a "marble palace," indeed formal, but very inviting.

For the evening gala, 295 guests start to arrive at 7:30 p.m. Reservations for this affair have been made days in advance. Expectations are high, for this is the first time the public will see and dine in the Hotel du Pont. The ladies are beautifully dressed in gowns purchased especially for this event, with lovely furs and jewelry. Their male escorts in evening attire add to the elegance of the evening.

Because of the crowds, the Hotel has to call upon the local police to keep the people moving. The visitors keep stopping to admire and comment on the magnificence of the architecture, the comfort and luxury. They are overwhelmed by the stunning ceiling in the Lobby and are captivated by the splendor.

As the guests approach the entrance to the Main Dining Room, they can hear the music from the string orchestra playing on the musicians' gallery. Voice levels drop in keeping with the volume of the music. The headwaiters and captains are unable to seat the guests, who are awed by the formality of the room. The waiters stand at their stations impeccably dressed, facing the guests. The tables are set with imported linen, the napkins folded as fans. A vase of freshly cut flowers and a band

[5] The silver was the second largest order ever received by a local Wilmington firm, Millard F. Davis. The largest was the silver service for the battleship *Delaware*.

*Private Dining Rooms*

*A corner of the Kitchen*

*The City Club Dining Room*

*The Lobby, 1920*

box with a bouquet for each lady are in place on each table.
The china, glass, and silver gleam in the soft light. The whole
effect is quiet and pleasing to the eye, suggesting luxury and
repose. Nothing detracts from the pleasure of the guests' first
impression.

Guests for reservations in the Grille Room are now backed
up in the Lobby. As they descend the roseal marble steps
wrapped in scagliola marble, they can hear the orchestra playing
for dancing after dinner. This room is much less formal than
the Main Dining Room. The guests pick up the beat of the
music. As they wait to be seated, they think they hear voices
coming from the tops of the massive oak columns from the
gnomes there who are playing cards, drinking beer, and chat-
ting to one another. The gnomes wink and say, "Come in, welcome, this is where we live. You are safe here. We will watch
over you, and we will enjoy this affair with you."

It is 10 p.m., and dinner is over. Dancing begins. The gala
is in its final stage. Guests are coming down from the Main
Dining Room to join in the fun, and visitors fill the area to
watch. The Grille is at this moment and will be for years to
come a social center for Delawareans. Some guests remain until
2 a.m. when they depart, happy and pleased. A voice says, "We
hope you had a good time, we did. Please come again. Good
night." Then the little gnomes fall asleep.

Now it is quiet, and the guests and visitors have all gone
home. Everyone has had nothing but praise for the Hotel. The
comments were thoughtful and warm, and the opening was
magnificent in every respect. Only one negative comment was
heard, from a lady who had called for a reservation for just one;
surely there would be a seat for her? She merely said, "I hope
they improve the reservations system." She had been standing
all evening.

All those who had played a part in putting it in place were
present that evening. The founders and the Du Pont Company
corporate executives were proud; the acceptance by the public

had exceeded their expectations. The architects, designers, engineers, and contractors felt this was one of their greatest moments; their craftsmanship showed at its finest. Political leaders realized the importance of the Hotel to the city and to the state and knew that it would serve in many ways as a property of dignity. The community was overwhelmed. The employees, the heartbeat of any hotel, were exhausted but very proud of their contributions. The training and preparation had been rewarding; they had performed as true professionals.

This day was a landmark for all Delawareans. From then on and for years to come, the Hotel du Pont would serve the business, social, and civic needs of the community.

# The City Club

The City Club was incorporated in Wilmington in February 1914 by a group of prominent businessmen headed by John J. Raskob, then treasurer of the Du Pont Company and one of the founders of the Hotel du Pont. The membership quickly grew to nearly six hundred residents and nonresidents, including Richard Patzowsky, vice president, who was president of the New Castle Leather Company and credited with being the originator of the club; Pierre S. du Pont and Ernest S. Taite; the executives of most major firms in the city; and business, banking, insurance, and civic leaders. Among the early members were John A. Montgomery, William W. Laird, Frank G. Tallman, Dr. J. A. Ellegood, J. P. Winchester, J. T. Skelly, Edward R. Pusey, George Frank Lord, B. B. Allen, and W. A. Simonton.

Space for the club was leased from the Hotel to provide a dining room, billiards room, cards room, reading room, and other appropriate facilities, all appointed with a homelike atmosphere. These rooms were on the eleventh floor adjacent to the Hotel's ballroom, which was used often by the club for dances and dinners.

In May 1915, a roof garden opened above the club's rooms. The Hotel then was the city's tallest building, and the new area provided a wonderful view embracing parts of four states. It was a delightful retreat in warm weather.

The roof garden was designed by Brown and Whiteside, local architects. They intended to reproduce the feeling of an Italian pavilion with its gardens, without following too minutely Italian motifs and details. J. A. Bader & Co., a well-known contracting firm in Wilmington, built the roof garden in just seven weeks, a remarkably short time considering the magnitude of the project.

Special afternoon teas and luncheons were provided for ladies in the families of members. Cards were issued permitting them to use the dining room in winter and the roof garden in summer. These areas could be reached directly by the building's elevators, so the ladies need not pass through the main quarters of the club. In the evening, an orchestra furnished music during dinner and later for dancing.

Unfortunately, this delightful and popular club was destined to be short-lived. It was housed, after all, in the corporate headquarters of the Du Pont Company, and pressing needs for office space arose. In 1918, R. R. M. Carpenter, on behalf of the firm, negotiated with and bought the assets of the City Club. While new clubs came into being to serve the needs of the membership, for years nothing seemed to replace the memory of the City Club in the community.

The City Club, although organized primarily for special purposes, gives every promise of developing into an organization which will play an important part in the expansion of the new Wilmington, just as it is playing an important part in the present upbuilding of this municipality. In fact, its beneficial influence not only is being felt in Wilmington, but throughout the peninsula . . .

In the case of the City Club one of the greatest reliefs to the whole architectural scheme is the magnificant view of Wilmington and its environments . . .

Visitors also are invariably impressed with the spirit of hospitality which pervades the club's quarters, and those who have been entertained there left with a warm spot in the heart for Wilmington in general and the City Club in particular.[6]

[6]*The Sunday Morning Star* (Wilmington), July 25, 1915.

# The Playhouse

The Playhouse Company was incorporated in April 1913 to construct and operate a theater in Wilmington. The men who provided the leadership to build the Playhouse were Pierre S. du Pont, John J. Raskob, and R. R. M. Carpenter. These men personally underwrote any losses in the early years. Mr. du Pont was an avid theatergoer, and on several occasions he purchased the entire seating of the theater to give the tickets to students for productions he thought they should see.

The construction of the theater, located within the walls of the Du Pont Building in what had been called Pinkett's Court, was a remarkable feat in 1913 and would be considered so even today.[7] Built in only 150 working days with more than a hundred men employed, it was fireproof, with three main entrances, eleven fire exits, and an enormous stage thirty-eight by eighty-five feet, larger than any of the New York theaters except the Hippodrome, the Metropolitan Opera House, and the Century Theater. The architect was Charles A. Rich of New York, and the builder was J. A. Bader & Co. of Wilmington. A problem arose when it was learned that the structural steel

[7] Information describing the Playhouse is taken largely from an article by Philip F. Crosland in the *Evening Journal* (Wilmington), October 10, 1973.

could not be delivered on time. The builders decided to use reinforced concrete girders to support the main roof and produced what would be the third largest concrete girder in the world (85 x 7½ x 2½ feet, weighing twelve tons). More than 12,000 pounds of concrete were poured each hour for nineteen hours to create this marvel.

Architecturally, the Playhouse was beautiful and spacious. From every point of view, the theater was one of the best appointed in the eastern part of the United States. Every detail was planned to ensure the audience the utmost in comfort and safety, with an aura of elegance. Crystal chandeliers hung in glittering cascades from the ceiling. The 1,200 seats were spaced so that no one need stand to allow another playgoer to enter a row; they were comfortable and wide enough to accommodate anyone regardless of his dimensions. The stage, acoustics, and large dressing rooms (and now air conditioning and lighting) made it a theater that lingered in the memory of the artist who enjoyed its splendor.

Opening night was October 15, 1913. Ticket lines began to form early that morning. The governor and mayor were among those in attendance to see *Bought and Paid For,* a sentimental melodrama by George Broadhurst. In the first program appeared an ad, *The Hotel du Pont, which also opened in 1913 (with European Plan rooms for $1.50 per day and up) is One of the Most Luxuriantly Appointed Hotels in America.* The critics wrote, "A successful opening."

Local events during that first season included the 27th commencement exercises of Goldey College, which graduated a class of 129 in November 1913. Other local groups were the Du Pont Puff and Powder Club, which presented *Patience;* Miss Kate McClafferty's dancing school, which gave student recitals; and the Employees Relief Association of Wilmington, which staged a minstrel show. An indication of the times was one play, *The Whip,* a spectacle requiring five special trains to transport scenery. The action included an automobile accident and a railroad wreck on stage, and live hounds and over one hundred players were in the production. The price to see top entertainment, such as Anna Pavlova, the great ballerina, was $3. Normal price ranges were from 25¢ in the balcony to $2.50 for box and orchestra seats. While motion pictures were in their infancy in 1913, films were shown in the Playhouse, including *Faust, Quo Vadis,* and *The Squaw Man.*

For nearly seventy years the Playhouse has had a meaningful effect on the cultural needs of the community. The famous of the theater world, playwrights, producers, directors, conductors, actors, actresses, and the finest entertainers have all appeared at the Playhouse. The presence of these great artists would mean that great performances would follow: Al Jolson on his knees singing, *Sonny Boy;* Sophie Tucker belting out, *What I Did for Your Father in World War I, I Can Do for You in World War II;* Rosalind Russell as *Auntie Mame;* Pearl Bailey in *Hello, Dolly;* Carol Channing in *Gentlemen Prefer Blondes;* Sir Harry Lauder; Mae West; Lauren Bacall; George Kaufman; Richard Rodgers; Oscar Hammerstein; John McCormick; Paul Robeson; Alfred Lunt and Lynn Fontanne; Charles Laughton and Elsa Lanchester; Raymond Massey; Tyrone Power; Sir Lawrence Olivier; Victor Borge; Marcel Marceau; magicians; ballet and dance troupes; grand and light opera; Shakespearean festivals; nearly all the big-name bands; and innumerable tryouts of plays and musicals on their way to Broadway.

The proximity of the Playhouse to New York is a real advantage for theater personnel. Few cities the size of Wilmington otherwise would have hoped to enjoy and be enriched by the talents of such great entertainers. With few exceptions, these artists are true professionals, indeed ladies and gentlemen. During their run the Hotel is their home away from home. Every need for accommodation is provided superbly for their comfort.

One might even say that the Playhouse and Hotel provided

the first dinner theater in Wilmington. Certainly it was planned that way when one observes the door in the Christina Room which opens into the lobby of the Playhouse. This arrangement, now discontinued, was used by playgoers to enjoy beverages and mingle with old friends during intermission. While the door has not been used for years, it might be well to reconsider its original intent.

Despite their obvious benefits to each other, the Hotel does not operate the Playhouse. The theater has its own manager, who reports directly to the General Services Department of the Du Pont Company. This has been the case for most of the history of the Playhouse, with the exception of several years during the late 1920s and early 1930s when it was run by the Shubert organization and renamed the Shubert Playhouse.

The theater occasionally is used for purposes other than the performing arts. The precedent was set in 1913 with the business college's graduation ceremonies. Political and civic meetings have taken place. The Du Pont Company holds its annual stockholders' meetings here.

The Playhouse exists today because of an extraordinary partnership between the Du Pont Company and the arts, formed sixty-eight years ago. Happily, this partnership is meaningful to the community as well.

# Expansion (1918–1919)

When the Hotel du Pont opened to the public in 1913, it was a master achievement in hotel architecture and ingenuity. It was believed to contain every facility for the entertainment and comfort of the people of Wilmington and the travelling public for years to come. A reporter from New York wrote, "Such a large hotel for such a small community."[8]

It soon became apparent that, despite the immensity of the floor space in the structure, the Hotel was too small to accommodate all the needs of the company and the business community. During 1918, plans were approved by the Du Pont Company to construct the fifth section of the Du Pont Building along 11th Street. These plans would include provisions for the expansion of the Hotel, adding a large new ballroom and 118 more guest rooms. The increase in facilities would nearly double the size of the Hotel. This project was completed and opened in 1919 and meant reevaluation of space utilization and guest services.

The first area to undergo change was the beautiful Rose

[8] Charles E. Geary, managing editor, *Hotel Review* (New York), January 15, 1913.

*Additional Hotel facilities incorporated into the fifth section of the Du Pont Building opened in 1919. Included were the new Lobby, the Gold Ballroom, the du Barry Room and 118 bedrooms.*

North facade of the Hotel du Pont showing addition on Eleventh Street. Note that the main entrance has been moved five bays westward. Photograph was taken in 1929. In the foreground is the excavation for First and Central Presbyterian Church.

*Colonial Room*

*Entrance to the Gold Ballroom Foyer*

*The du Barry Room in the 1920s*

Room, the French salon reserved for the ladies; it would become the new Lobby. Guests and employees reading the announcement of this proposal were stunned and did not believe that any change could possibly be considered. Just a few years ago, at the opening of the Hotel, thousands stopped and stood in amazement at its magnificence. As renovations started, workmen wondered how it was possible to disturb such beauty and elegance. Many years later, Irving S. Shapiro, then chairman of the board and chief executive officer of the Du Pont Company, looked at an old photograph of the Rose Room and commented, "They did things right in those days."

The architecture of the new Lobby would be in keeping with the plans established in 1911. It would be elegant, homelike, and comfortable. The wooden inlaid floors became marble, the mirrored walls replaced with imported travertine stone; the original ceiling, bathed by lights from crystal chandeliers, was changed to complement the ceilings of the Green Room and new Ballroom Suite. The design of the ceiling closely followed those of the Ducal Palace in Venice. This sculptured ceiling, with carved rosettes and scrolls, was finished in gold, blue, and red.

The entrance from the Lobby to the Ballroom Suite would be a masterful achievement in design. Two handcarved American walnut doors, twelve feet high, were hung on an imported roseal marble frame sculpted in basket weave patterns. This doorway provided a marvel of beauty for guests who admired the delicate handcarving. To the left of these doors stood a tall clock purchased in 1918 through Herbert R. Stone from one of New York's finest furniture galleries. It was made by Elliott in England. The handcarved case, finished in walnut and mahogany veneers, weighed more than 400 pounds. The carvings were influenced by English, German, and French motifs. The movement was cable wound with a nine tube triple chime of Whittington, St. Michael's, and Westminster. At one time this masterpiece was moved from the Lobby, and rumors had it for sale. Happily today it stands again in the Lobby and is enjoyed and admired by thousands of guests.[9]

The floors were covered by imported Oriental rugs. All furniture was custom made and upholstered in tapestry and velvet. Two unusually large blue and white urns were placed by the travertine columns. They are gone now, but someday it is hoped they will reappear.

In one corner of the Lobby would be a door leading downstairs to the health club. Over the door was embossed: *Fi du Plaisir Que la Crainte Peut Corrompre,* meaning, "I don't care for pleasure if I have worries at the same time." On April 3, 1917, the plans and drawings were submitted to build one of the most complete health clubs for any hotel at that time. The facilities would include massage, steam, hot, and rubbing rooms; waiting and dressing rooms; a barber shop; and a large swimming pool, to be located under the new Gold Ballroom. A small portion of this plan was approved. Archery experts and a golf pro were available for lessons; nets were arranged to provide a driving range. Happily, the swimming pool was not constructed, since swimming pools do not attract guests in a downtown hotel and are expensive to maintain.

The first Lobby would now become the Hotel's Soda Shop. How could this room, two and a half stories high, of marble, with scagliola columns, a fireplace, mosaic and terrazzo floors, now undergo change? Both employees and guests must have said, "This will be the most beautiful and expensive soda shop in the world!" The original entrance to this Lobby now became a fashionable ladies' hat shop.

In July 1955, the Soda Shop was displaced. Plans were made to better utilize the space in and around it. The major undertaking dealt with the high ceiling, and a slab was run across the Lobby at first floor level to make room for additional offices. The ground floor provided space for a jeweler, florist, airline

[9] Descriptive information on the clock was furnished by Samuel H. Achuff, a noted clock specialist in Wilmington.

reservations center, shops, and offices. During this construction, a foyer was designed for the Green Room. The hallway of terrazzo and mosaic floors was replaced by Tennessee marble, and other areas were carpeted over.

The newly created Colony Club was located on the second floor, overlooking the Playhouse and Pinkett's Court where a blind alley ran halfway through the block toward 11th Street. It was a private club used by members as a meeting place, for reading and relaxation. One could look from the club directly into the dressing rooms of the Playhouse entertainers. Bellmen who were not members of the club were quick to learn of this unsatisfactory condition. It is understood that two bellmen were terminated for having a view of the entertainers without tickets. In time, the area became a private dining room.

This project caused a lot of controversy. However, after completion, everyone seemed pleased with the results. The alterations provided much needed space and were most attractive architecturally.

*An intricately detailed bronze stairrail highlights
the entrance to the Gold Ballroom suite*

*The Gold Ballroom, about 1920*

*he Du Pont Soda Shop in 1927*

*The Hat Shop in the 1920s*

*Heartbeat:*
*People to People*

# Organization: A Chronology

### 1912, JULY 2

A corporation, the Hotel Du Pont Co., was organized to operate the hotel. The executives of this company were Pierre S. du Pont, president, and John J. Raskob, secretary-treasurer. These two men would have corporate responsibility for the Hotel du Pont.

### 1912, AUGUST 14

Ernest S. Taite was employed as the first manager while the Hotel still was being built. He was recognized as an outstanding hotel executive, since he had managed several of the finest hotels in the country. Arriving directly from the Hotel Astor in New York, he assumed the duty as consultant to the Hotel Du Pont Co. on affairs concerning construction, furnishing, equipment, and staffing. Prior to the opening, Mr. Taite brought to Wilmington a number of hotel professionals from other hotels as staff and to hire and train new employees.

### 1913, JANUARY 15

The Hotel officially opened for business. Mr. Taite not only experienced the problems of opening the Hotel but was affected greatly by the impact of World War I and the plans already under consideration for expanding the Hotel, in fact, to nearly double its size. In addition, managing the new City Club was no easy task. One of his most difficult adjustments would be the monitoring of the Hotel's performance by the officers of the Hotel Du Pont Co. He resigned on June 6, 1921.

### 1921, JUNE 6

Harry J. Harkins became the second manager of the Hotel. He was a Wilmingtonian who had worked at the Clayton House at 5th and Market Streets. He was considered a folksy manager, very low key, not nearly as formal as Mr. Taite. He was nice to everyone. During his administration, an arrangement was entered into with the Boomer–T. Coleman du Pont group to explore the feasibility of this company's merging with the Hotel. This arrangement was terminated within three months, and Mr. Harkins remained as manager until he resigned at the end of 1926 to become general manager of the Penn Harris Hotel in Harrisburg, Pennsylvania.

### 1927, JANUARY 1

The Hotel du Pont leased to the Bowman-Biltmore chain the operation of the Hotel, and its name was changed to the Hotel du Pont-Biltmore. Charles W. Gibbs, a highly regarded and experienced manager with the Bowman-Biltmore chain, became the third manager of the Hotel until his death in June 1933. He was respected by the employees, maintained high standards, and was considered fair and demanding. During the Bowman-Biltmore administration the Hotel deteriorated badly. Money for project requests for renovations was not made available to Mr. Gibbs by Bowman-Biltmore, and it soon became a second-rate hotel.

A provision of the lease was that Bowman-Biltmore would divide the profits with the Hotel Du Pont Co. Should there be a loss, the Hotel Du Pont Co. would absorb it. This unwise arrangement was puzzling, since Pierre S. du Pont played a role in it and was considered one of the financial geniuses of his time.

## 1933, JUNE 30

The agreement with the Bowman-Biltmore Hotels Corporation was cancelled by mutual consent, and the Hotel's name reverted to Hotel du Pont. From June 30 until November 1, 1933, the Hotel was managed by Assistant Manager Henry Shreffler.

## 1933, NOVEMBER 1

Frank C. Gregson became the fourth manager. His career began in hotels located in North Carolina, Tennessee, Virginia, and New York. He came to the Hotel du Pont from the Lexington Hotel in New York. Affectionately known as "Frank," he was a highly trained and respected hotel professional and was known in the community as a real Southern gentleman. Mr. Gregson directed the Hotel du Pont for nineteen years.

## 1934, JUNE 30

The Hotel Du Pont Co. was dissolved, and its assets (except cash) and liabilities were sold to the Du Pont Building Corp.

## 1936, SEPTEMBER 30

The Du Pont Building Corp. was dissolved and its assets and business transferred to E. I. du Pont de Nemours & Co. (Inc.). The Hotel now became a division of the company, reporting to the Office Buildings Department, later to be named the General Services Department.

At this point it may be well to review briefly what transpired during the administration of the Hotel Du Pont Co. covering the initial period of twenty-three years. The primary objectives set forth by the founders were accomplished. But the tremendous growth of the Du Pont Company, World War I, the expansion of the Hotel's facilities, the passage and repeal of the

Prohibition Act, the stock market crash, and the Depression all would have a profound effect on the operation of the Hotel. During this period, too, the four managers would feel regularly the involvement of the officers of the Hotel Du Pont Co. in day-to-day operations. While each one understood this, it was not an easy arrangement, particularly for highly trained, experienced hotel professionals.

From a review of old records, reports, letters, and appropriations requests, it is clear that the officers of the Hotel Du Pont Co. were in full control of the Hotel du Pont. This meant not only executive accountability but also operating responsibility. One important facet of this control was complete cooperation to develop the most meaningful and effective organization for the future. And one cannot overlook the fact that one of the officers, Pierre S. du Pont, maintained a suite in the Hotel from 1913 until his death in 1954. During that period, his very presence would have a direct and meaningful impact on the Hotel operation.

### 1953, MAY 1

John D. La Mothe became the fifth manager and continued in that capacity for fifteen years. He was the first manager who had worked previously in various areas of responsibility within the Du Pont Company. As one of his many assignments, he was assistant manager of the Hotel du Pont from 1945 to 1949. He was recognized in the hotel industry for his leadership and established the Educational Institute of the American Hotel & Motel Association. Mr. La Mothe was a refined gentleman of the highest order, admired and respected in the community, where he was active in the American Red Cross and Boy Scouts, and by all his employees. They remember him for his deep concern with employee relations.

### 1968, APRIL 1

Harry V. Ayres became the sixth manager, for a term of ten years. He was the second manager to come from within the

Du Pont Company, as he transferred from the Personnel and Industrial Relations Division of the General Services Department. He first was assigned to several positions within the Hotel du Pont, including Food and Beverage manager and assistant manager, before becoming manager in 1968. During this period, Mr. Ayres was also president of the Delaware Hotel-Motel Association, director of the American Hotel & Motel Association, and a member of its Executive Committee. He was also chairman of its Employee Relations Committee. While involved in community affairs, his primary concern was the expansion of Red Clay Creek Presbyterian Church (established in 1722). He always was concerned for the staff, the image of the Hotel, its history, and its architectural restoration.

### 1978, OCTOBER 1

Ferdinand Wieland, a native of Salzburg, Austria, became the seventh and current manager. Before joining the Hotel du Pont in 1967, he gained his professional knowledge in European and American hotels and restaurants, including three Swiss hotels: the Elite in Bienne, the Beau Rivage Palace in Lausanne, and the Gstaad Palace in Gstaad. He was also employed by Holland-America Lines. During these many assignments he became fluent in five languages. His Hotel du Pont duties, over a period of six years, included captain of the Dining Rooms, Banquet sales representative, manager of Food Services, Food and Beverage manager, assistant manager, and manager.

Mr. Wieland is a member of the Rotary Club of Wilmington and serves on the board of directors for the Delaware Chapter of the American Red Cross. He is also a member of numerous committees of the American Hotel & Motel Association. Certainly he will sense and be inspired by the dedication of those who came before him.

# The Guests

The Hotel du Pont had just opened when a large number of requests were received for permanent residences. This unexpected development would mean that a large number of rooms planned to accommodate transient guests would not be available. For example, Pierre S. du Pont, who established his residence in the Hotel in 1913, would require four or five rooms; Mr. and Mrs. John J. Raskob wanted three rooms which were to be occupied during the winter months. Nearly twenty other applications asked for suites. These requests came from many well-to-do elderly citizens of the community who could afford the cost and did not wish to maintain their big houses. They would bring with them furniture, glass, and silver, and many other keepsakes, which gave each suite an individual and homelike atmosphere. In a sense, the Hotel filled a social need, since there were no existing full care living facilities for the prosperous elderly during this period.

These permanent guests were delightful. They appreciated their independence and were generous and kind to the employees. Some of the gifts given to the staff included $5.00 and $2.50 gold pieces, yards of fabric, jewelry, candy, perfume, and tickets to the Playhouse. As time moved forward, many became paternalistic and demanded service that had not been planned for. Some employees objected to demands for personal care. The residents objected to increases in rent, which worried Mr. du Pont, and he expressed his concern for those on fixed incomes. During one substantial increase in rent, he wrote to the manager of the Hotel, "I think you are trying to push me out through the roof!"

Many permanent residents would not permit inspection of their suites and, if they were entertaining, would not even allow the housekeeper on the floor. Still others would go so far as to reprimand overnight Hotel guests. Some actually fed the pigeons from their rooms, despite the incompatibility of pigeons and downtown office buildings. One guest left his window open while he was away, and a pigeon promptly moved in and established a nest. When the gentleman returned, he asked to be moved to another suite until the family had hatched. His request was denied.

One elderly lady fell in her room and was heard calling for help. Responding to the call, it was learned she had installed five locks on the beautiful mahogany door, with no way to enter other than to break it down. A bellman, who admired these old doors, suggested he go to the floor above and, if her window were open, be lowered to the balcony and on into the room. While not in keeping with safety regulations, it worked. The bellman said, "I'm sure happy we were able to save that door!" In all probability what he meant to say was, "I am happy we could help the guest and save the door too."

One gentleman, a retired chemist, moved into the Hotel and brought with him a canopy bed and other furniture. He also had a refrigerator delivered to his suite. During a routine room inspection, the refrigerator was found with a chain around it with a big lock attached. His knowledge of chemistry had been used to make bathtub gin. A housekeeper commented, "I hope he is a better chemist than he is a gin maker." He moved out in a short time.

The 1929 Wall Street Crash could be heard reverberating throughout the Hotel. One guest lost $6 million in one week. Others were losing $100,000 an hour, and so it went. Many who had previously tipped $10 to $15 for room service now found it difficult to find a dime. Many residents moved out bag and baggage. The biggest catastrophe of all was well on its way, and entries in the guest book began to fade: World War II was on.

During this period, a policy was established that no further permanent guests would be accepted. This policy would not affect those currently residing in the Hotel. The late James Farley, Cabinet member during the Roosevelt administration and later chairman of the board of the Coca-Cola Company's international operations, came to Wilmington for corporate meetings and to see his old friend, the late Ralph Hayes, who resided in the Hotel and was its last permanent guest. Mr. Farley called the Hotel one day and asked for Mr. Hayes, adding, "I know he is not out pursuing the ladies, because he is the same age as I am, and I gave that up long ago!"

The end of the permanent residences closed a memorable relationship meaningful to so many guests who had lived in dignity. It was an unforgettable experience for the Hotel.

An historic problem in the Hotel has been low occupancy during weekends and holidays. The business traveller checked in on Monday and out on Friday. The sales manager committed himself to improving this condition by developing a tour business, with the objective of increasing weekend and holiday occupancy by twenty-five percent. This increase would have no significant impact on labor costs.

It was necessary first for him to gather information on such concerns as potential, the advertising budget, local attractions, the whole tour package, cost, guides, geographic areas covered, and personal contact, and to review with Hotel supervision what would be required in the rooms and in the food facilities. Areas of responsibility were put in place. With little experience and a great deal to be learned, the program was initiated.

What have been the results? During 1965, the first year, just three buses came, representing only 150 guests. From this modest beginning, the Hotel learned important details, including the fact that nearly ninety-five percent of the tourists were women, more twin-bedded rooms were required, dining room schedules for these visitors were altered, and special menus created certain problems. Each group had to be welcomed on arrival and thanked for coming before departure. Essentially, all these guests were retirees, well-travelled, and delightful.

On one occasion, a number of ladies called on the manager. "We are on a tour of your area, and this is our fourth visit. Our ages average seventy-five years. Most of us have been widows for a long time, and we have travelled together all over our country, Europe, and the Caribbean. We really came to tell you how much we enjoy this beautiful and luxurious hotel. Thank you for the warm welcome and the dignity and, yes, the love we feel. It is a memorable experience for all of us. Thank you and all your staff." They departed quietly. It was a visit that will always be remembered.

During Christmas, the Hotel is beautifully decorated. The festivities generate an excitement for this special season. All of the guest rooms are filled with tour groups to enjoy a holiday away from home. One year these guests, nearly all ladies, with a few men here and there, filled the Lobby. The manager stopped by to wish them all a happy holiday and a Merry Christmas. One gracious lady spoke up, "I am eighty-five years old. Do you know what it means to sit here and feel the majesty of this moment and be a part of it? Why, it makes you wonder why this does not happen all around the world!" A gentleman with the group remarked, "Young man, that was nice of you, your sentiments are appreciated. How would you like to travel with thirty women on a bus for several weeks? I must tell you, I am eighty-seven years old, and I still enjoy it!" Everyone laughed along with him. It was Christmas, and a special moment for them and for the manager.

Today, the objective has been reached and now requires an

up-to-date report. During 1979, 8,000 guests arrived by bus, and many of these counted this as their tenth visit. There were 2,000 others unable to obtain reservations because of prior commitments made by the Hotel. Our state and surrounding areas should be proud of all the attractions; the guests are delighted with them. The sales manager's program has been an outstanding achievement. This experience in tour business has been advantageous both to the Hotel du Pont and to the community.

During the Hotel's history, the primary objective, to serve the total business community, has received the highest priority. While there are exceptions, these business visitors usually stay only one or two nights. Nearly forty percent of the Hotel's guest list is Du Pont Company related. Interviews and surveys have been conducted to determine the adequacy of the services provided for this large segment of the Hotel's business.

In summary, they have proved that the needs are basic and simple: a quiet, comfortable room. Those guests who come often also appreciate being recognized by staff members and assigned to their favorite rooms. This attention is very special to them. They also require dependable wake-up and message service with no delays, prompt breakfast service, and, if necessary, prompt and efficient cleaning and pressing service. A room should be available for baggage after check-out time and, because they travel light, no bellman is required in or out. Since they come often, they request accurate information on community events and transportation. Above all, under no circumstances are they taken for granted.

The Guaranteed Room Rate Plan was established by the Hotel some years ago. National hotel and motel chains were called upon by the Hotel du Pont to negotiate room rates for Du Pont Company employees travelling on company business. The 1980 *Hotel-Motel Corporate Rate Directory* was distributed to 12,500 Du Pont Company employees. Estimated savings in company travel expenses now exceed a half million dollars each year.

The growth in international travel has increased tenfold during the last few years, and the services provided for these travellers have been expanded as well. Many helpful aids now are provided: menus and room information printed in five languages, currency exchange information, multilingual employees, identified electrical outlets, a list of interpreters, a variety of foreign language magazines, community and emergency information, green tea for visitors from the Far East, and shortwave radios. A little national flag for the country of the guest is placed in his room during his stay. An entire floor has been set aside as the international floor.

During the last few years, there has been a major increase also in women travellers. These visitors set forth a number of specific requirements: when they entertain a client, they expect to receive the check (women tip as well or better than men); they do not wish to be seated in the center of the dining room; their bedrooms must be well-lighted and located near the elevators; they want *Vogue* and comparable magazines and information on local boutiques. They appreciate a bud vase of flowers in their room. In essence, they merely wish to be treated like any other visitor.

Increased emphasis has been placed on services required by handicapped persons. Rooms are now available which have been designed by representatives of the handicapped and are engineered to meet their special needs. Braille for the blind is now used in each elevator to identify each floor, and chimes notify the sightless that the elevator doors are closing. The use of guide dogs must be understood, and these wonderful animals are permitted in the dining rooms. Courses train Hotel employees to effectively assist the handicapped.

Several major league baseball clubs have roomed at the Hotel. Among these athletes were the Philadelphia Phillies and the New York Yankees. Joe DiMaggio was then only twenty years old. Young boys and girls came in great numbers to meet the players and collect autographs. Many of the negotiations for the purchase of the Phillies by R. R. M. Carpenter for his son, Bob, took place there.

Governors' and mayors' regional conferences have been held in the Hotel. Such meetings involve increased security, press facilities, and staff accommodations. You can very easily pick out the guest who is running for office, particularly if he is hoping to move up in the political arena. His staff and press corps will be larger, he will be called frequently from meetings for telephone calls, with a lot of whispering on the side with colleagues, and he will always be in the right place with the right people. The Hotel staff rarely misses in making its own selections. During an election year, the Hotel is like an election center, with many national figures arriving who will rarely stop again until the next four years.

Several years ago, seventeen Japanese governors and their wives were invited by Governor Elbert Carvel to visit Delaware. There was quite a contrast in height between the small Japanese and Governor Carvel, who is 6'7" tall. Each visiting governor was provided with an automobile and driver during his visit. The preparation for their arrival at the Hotel was a challenge, especially in the field of communications, since none of the guests spoke English. Information booklets were printed in Japanese, as indeed were all the schedules and arrangements. Japanese interpreters were present to handle telephone calls which the Hotel employees called the Japanese hotline. Newspapers in Japanese were also made available. The Hotel was proud to have been a part of this occasion which honored our city and state.

Some months later, the doorman reported that a beautiful white stallion, which had belonged to the emperor of Japan, was requesting a reservation. The desk clerk took care of this matter. The horse, whose lovely Japanese name meant White Frost, left for a visit to the racetrack at Delaware Park. Later in the day, a cancellation was received. The horse decided he would be more comfortable at Delaware Park. We agreed.

Six mayors from the leading cities of Poland were invited by Wilmington's Mayor John Babiarz to visit Delaware. Many of the employees of the Hotel were of Polish descent, and some of their families had been born in those cities. Mayor Babiarz, a Polish-American himself, introduced the mayors to a number of the employees, which was a rewarding and emotional experience for all of them.

Some years ago, the great Ignace Paderewski came to the Playhouse and spent the night in the Hotel. A piano had been put in his suite, and after the Playhouse concert Paderewski retired to his room, accompanied by Walter Bacon of Claymont who was the manager of Paderewski's first American tour. They rehashed the concert and Mr. Bacon, who himself was quite a pianist, got into a heated discussion with the maestro. One word led to another. The maestro went to the piano while Mr. Bacon stomped up and down the room shouting, "More pedal, Mr. Paderewski, more pedal!" Apparently, some of the other guests in the Hotel were disturbed by what they thought was mere piano banging and complained to management. But the night clerk did not have the nerve to transmit these complaints to the world famous musician. The irritated guests had to grit their teeth and endure what they thought was noise but what was probably the most unusual musical discussion that ever took place in Wilmington.[1]

During World War II, a number of Ferry Command pilots lived at the Hotel. The officer in charge was Captain Barry Goldwater. Of the ten pilots registered, eight were considered very wealthy, which may not have been a qualification for membership. They were here to fly aircraft from the New Castle Airport to overseas bases. During Christmas, Captain Goldwater asked a Hotel staff member to escort him in order to meet the employees and give them gifts, which were quite generous. We wonder now whether the captain was making his plans for a

[1] As reported by Bill Frank in the *Wilmington Morning News*, January 6, 1961.

future venture into politics. The captain was highly respected by all the employees, and the Hotel was honored to host this distinguished group.

It was not long before another war hero would visit the Hotel while he looked into the possibilities of becoming president of the United States: Senator John F. Kennedy. Mrs. Kennedy, who accompanied him, was said to be as shy as the senator was forceful.

One of the most asked questions is, who is the most important guest to visit the Hotel? Without any hesitation, it is always the President of the United States. Eight presidents have visited the Hotel during its history. It may be of interest to know what planning is necessary before such a visit. Days prior to the president's arrival, two Secret Service agents come to the Hotel. They introduce themselves, show their identification, and then are introduced to Hotel management. They discuss the time of arrival, transportation, what door the president will enter and leave by, who will greet him, whether he will need a suite, its location, its exits, the number of other rooms on the floor, whether he will be accompanied, and if so, by whom. One key person on the Hotel staff is assigned for coordination. Special identification is given to those employees permitted to serve the president. The Secret Service notifies five law enforcement agencies.

During the president's visit, all regular guests in the Hotel are checked daily. The traffic pattern will be established which the president will walk, and any room he is to visit is checked out daily. If he is to have food service, the necessary precautions are taken. Communications must be put in place for the duration, and press facilities set up. Any special needs of the president are arranged for in advance. The Secret Service agents are highly professional and are comfortable to work with. They depart with the president. Such a visit is truly an exceptional one for any community and hotel.

Through the portals of the Hotel have passed a cavalcade of

prominent people that is world embracing; the guest list is daz-
zling. They could variously be described as private, very formal,
eccentric, friendly, comfortable to be with, interesting, rich in
knowledge, with leadership qualities, a sense of humor, and
charisma. Would it not be of interest to set forth some names
of guests who created excitement by their visits?

William H. Taft—Warren G. Harding—Herbert Hoover—Harry S. Truman
—John F. Kennedy—Richard Nixon—Gerald R. Ford—Jimmy Carter

Nelson A. Rockefeller—Hubert H. Humphrey—Alben Barkley—Spiro
Agnew—Barry Goldwater

Elliot Richardson—Henry Kissinger—James A. Farley—Joseph Sisco—
Alfred E. Smith—Christian Herter

King Carl XVI Gustaf and Prince Bertil of Sweden—Prince Rainier of
Monaco—Prince Carlos Hugo and Princess Irene of Spain—The Earl of
Wemyss and Lady Wemyss of Scotland

Douglas MacArthur—Leslie Groves—William Westmoreland—Alexander
Haig

Richard E. Byrd—William F. Halsey—Raymond A. Spruance—C. R.
Rosenthal

Norman Rockwell—the Wyeths—John McCoy—Frank Schoonover—
Alexander Stuart—Charles Parks

Amelia Earhart—Elinor Smith—Wiley Post—Charles Lindbergh—Alan
Shepard

Red Grange—Jesse Owens—William Tilden—Jack Dempsey—By
Saam—Kyle Rote—Bowie Kuhn—Bob Carpenter—Pete Rose—Randy
White—Pete Rozelle—Bert Bell—Eddie Arcaro

Frank Howard, Clemson—Ara Parseghian, Notre Dame—Darrell Royal,
Texas—Jack Curtis, California—Dave Nelson, Delaware

Cardinal Shehan—Rev. Jesse Jackson—Rev. Leon Sullivan—Bishop
Fulton J. Sheen—Father Tucker, private chaplain for Prince Rainier

John L. Lewis—Jimmy Hoffa—James Mitchell

Guy Lombardo—Vincent Lopez—Paul Whiteman—Fred Waring—Duke
Ellington—Lester Lanin—Meyer Davis—Jimmy and Tommy Dorsey—
Efrem Zimbalist

Oscar Hammerstein—George Kaufman—Richard Rodgers—George M.
Cohan—Eugene O'Neill—Sigmund Romberg

Robert Goulet—Bob Hope—Gene Autry—Gregory Peck—Rex Harrison—
Ricardo Montalban—Edward G. Robinson—Lena Horne—Elizabeth

Taylor—Claudette Colbert—Anne Baxter—Katharine Hepburn—Gloria Swanson—Bette Davis—Constance Bennett—Ginger Rogers—Fred and Adele Astaire—Boris Karloff—Dorothy Gish—Gertrude Lawrence—Barbara BelGeddes—Tallulah Bankhead—Katherine Cornell—Ethel Merman—José Ferrer—Elsa Lanchester—Barry Fitzgerald—Miriam Hopkins

Alfred P. Sloan—the Du Ponts—Robert Woodruff—Thomas A. Murphy—the Fisher brothers—Irving S. Shapiro—William Durant—James Conant—Crawford H. Greenewalt—Ruth Patrick

Eleanor Roosevelt—Patricia Nixon—Rosalynn Carter—Mrs. Alben Barkley—Jacqueline Kennedy—Ethel Kennedy—Mrs. Marshall Field—Emily P. Bissell—Elizabeth S. Post

This list does not include governors or mayors attending conferences, or ambassadors and consuls general from many countries. Nor is it possible, because of the hundreds of companies incorporated in Delaware, to list the boards of directors of these companies. Also, the managers and players of five major league baseball clubs are too numerous to list.

These celebrities, together with business men and women, tour travellers, and overnight visitors, make the mixture of guests a delightful and ever fascinating one for the Hotel. It is a pleasure to serve them all.

# The Staff

The most beautiful hotel in the world is just that, until it is staffed. The employees are the character and personality of the property, indeed its very reputation. All must understand that their primary reason for employment is to serve the guest, and at all times they must provide cheerful and efficient service. Each member of the organization must understand both his or her individual responsibility and how his or her commitment relates to fellow employees. Nothing justifies pride in a hotel more than the performance of the staff.

The Hotel du Pont has 490 employees: 215 men and 275 women. Stability and longevity of service have long been characteristics of the staff. Management's concern for minorities in employment and opportunity received high priority many years ago. Today, more than forty percent of the employees fall in this category. Staff services such as accounting, purchasing, engineering, and maintenance are bought from other divisions of the Du Pont Company's General Services Department.

During the period from the opening in 1913 until 1939, employees of the Hotel were not eligible to participate in the employee benefit plans and general advances in salaries and wages adopted by the Du Pont Company. After the Hotel Du Pont Co.

was dissolved in 1936, the employees were classified as regular employees of the parent company and were made eligible for all benefits and advances adopted by the Du Pont Company. The participation of Hotel employees in these general wage advances and benefit plans would increase the operating cost of the Hotel du Pont by approximately $75,000 per year.

At that time, no hotel in this country treated its employees with such liberality. Supporting this position was General Kincaid, president of the American Hotels Corporation, and the management of the Waldorf-Astoria, one of the most noted hotels in the industry for fair treatment of employees.

Surveys made today for comparison of benefit plans and wages show that employees of the Hotel du Pont compare favorably with the highest paying hotels in the world. This rating is most helpful in selecting quality employees, reduces turnover, and has a definite effect on the continuity of quality.

Surprising as it may seem, the Hotel must develop eighteen specific job descriptions that outline in detail the skills and duties for each position. In other words, to provide the services required for each guest, eighteen trained employees are needed. These include the telephone operator, reservations clerk, doorman, guest registration clerk, bellman, guest room inspectress, housekeeper-houseman, maintenance man, valet, room service waiter, chef in food preparation, headwaiter-captain, checkroom attendant, waitress, waitress assistant, bartender, representative of management, and cashier. This list excludes two other important aspects of guest relations: parking and transportation. While these are not a part of the Hotel's organization, a close follow-up on these two services is maintained.

The employees in each area receive extensive training and are proud of their accomplishments; they will not tolerate criticism from other areas. Should a breakdown in service occur, no effort or time is spent on the question of whom to blame, but rather why it happened and what is necessary to prevent a recurrence. While individualism prevails in each group, collectively all are dedicated to providing an exciting and satisfactory experience for the guest.

An information board is provided to post all comments from guests. Each month an employee is selected by the guests and by his fellow employees as the one contributing most to good guest relations. His name is engraved on a plaque and displayed in the Lobby. At the end of the year, the same process is followed to select the employee of the year.

In such a diversified organization, communication must take the highest priority. The Hotel manager and his staff meet each morning to review and discuss all the activities from the previous day and to plan ahead for the next day. Each year the manager meets with all employees in small groups to review the previous year's performance, answer any questions, and outline how each one fits into the plans for the following year. A monthly newsletter is prepared for all employees which sets forth detailed information on what is happening throughout the Hotel.

It is fair to say that the Hotel du Pont enjoys a reputation of excellence in the community and throughout the hotel industry around the world. If this is true, and it is, then it is an outstanding credit to all employees of the Hotel over the years who have made it possible. There is something about the Hotel that affects those who work there.

Once a year, the manager invites all retirees to an informal luncheon to reminisce and talk about the good old days. This affair involves nearly 115 former employees who have contributed so much to the Hotel's outstanding reputation. Service in this group covers a period from fifteen through forty-four years, or an average of twenty-five years per employee. As the retirees arrive, they are eager to discuss old experiences. Everyone appears happy, all are talking at the same time, with lots of laughter; no one seems to be listening. "Do you remember?" "Yes, I remember." Let's listen in.

"I was around here for forty-four years, spanned two wars,

five managerial administrators. There were many highlights. Why, during the Depression, our small pay was reduced twice. Times were difficult. Then, do you know what happened? A new room manager arrived and in a short time, with no notice, he terminated six of us girls. In those days, there was no unemployment compensation, and no other jobs were available. Well, I got word to Mr. Pierre, and the next day those terminations were cancelled with instructions that no such action in the future would be taken without his approval. We never forgot Mr. du Pont for that!"

"There's Mr. Nielsen, the maitre d'; it was rare indeed for anyone to call him Max. He ate his sandwich with a knife and fork, and no one dared pour his coffee."

"I will never forget the headwaiter who was given a $250 tip just for himself, and he divided it with all of us. He was a special headwaiter!"

"Did you ever see the Du Ponts dance? Why, they would be a credit to Broadway! They played pretty good music, also."

"Boy, did I get a going over for paging a Du Pont in the dining room. It was a no-no! I just didn't know any better."

"Those Irish and Polish girls who worked in the laundry room were beautiful and so nice. That area was off limits for us bellmen. Do you remember? I sure do!"

"I looked after Conrad Hilton and his executives. During a visit, he told me he wished all of his hotels were as nice as the Du Pont. He was a nice gentleman. After keeping the Green Room open for dinner beyond the normal schedule, son Nicky complained about the prices! Can you imagine that?"

"Al Smith sure came a lot. You could pick him out with that cigar and derby. It was during the election and he was trying to get some money together. He was a great friend of J. J. Raskob."

"Did you know that supervision nipped in those days?"

"World War I ended with some celebration! People were proud of their country then."

"One time a guest called to have his suit pressed. He went through all the pockets and asked that it be ready in three hours. While walking down the hallway, I saw three $1,000 bills drop out of a pocket. I didn't know such a thing existed! I gave the money to the manager to be returned. All employees were excited. The next day in the newspaper, 'Bellman Finds $3,000—$10 Richer!' "

"Room service food, after midnight, was purchased from a nearby restaurant on Orange Street. We charged the guest Hotel prices, making a good bit of money. I was never asked about the markup!"

"I remember the Franklin Roosevelt, Jr. and Ethel du Pont dinner party in the Gold Ballroom. Not many Roosevelts came to the Hotel. I know President Roosevelt did not."

"I'll never forget the flu epidemic. The whole community worked together. There were many sick guests in the Hotel."

"What about those big snowstorms? Lots of us would walk blocks and blocks to the Hotel when it was too snowy to drive. Other restaurants and businesses closed down, but not ours. The customers were already there!"

Stories went on and on, such as finding $500 in cash under a table in the Gold Ballroom or a $35,000 diamond brooch.

Several times within a month the employees reported seeing a man, who was not a Hotel guest, going from room to room to play any of the six pianos owned by the Hotel. Whenever he was challenged, he said he had been given permission by the manager to practice. The manager, of course, had never heard of him. At last, he was approached while he was playing in the empty Gold Ballroom. He became very indignant and said that whenever he stayed at the Waldorf-Astoria management always put a baby grand piano in his suite. He was told in no uncertain terms that he was not a guest of the Hotel and that if he were ever caught playing there again his suite at the city jail would not be large enough to accommodate so much as a piano bench.

Basil Rathbone asked a bellman to buy him four pairs of

shoes. He specified the size and color and stated they were to be the finest available. The bellman returned from his shopping tour very proud of his purchases. Mr. Rathbone was complimentary and liked the shoes but decided to give them to the bellman, and to his surprise, they fit the bellman perfectly. The bellman said, "I had the most expensive and best-dressed feet for the next few years."

Blackstone, the great sleight of hand magician, called the valet to clean and press his tuxedo, the most complex suit the valet had ever seen. The number of pockets and special compartments was a revelation in itself. The suit was cleaned and pressed and returned promptly; however, Mr. Blackstone's aide misplaced it. With all of Blackstone's magic, he could not pull the suit out of a hat! Twenty minutes before curtain time, the valet was paged in a nearby theater to report to the Playhouse. The valet's magic worked; the tuxedo was located, and the show went on.

Paul Whiteman, the king of jazz, had driven down from New York in an open automobile wearing a fur coat. On arrival at the Hotel, Mr. Whiteman noticed that his diamond ring was missing. The bellman standing nearby said, "Would you mind if I search your car? It was cold today, and your fingers may have contracted." The bellman did find the ring; the diamond was the size of his thumb and must have been worth a fortune. When he notified Mr. Whiteman that the ring had been found, the musician dropped the telephone. The bellman was given a $1 tip. Seven years later, Mr. Whiteman was in the Hotel again, remembered the bellman, and gave him $100. The bellman said, "That was real thoughtful of him."

The noted lawyer, Clarence Darrow, was in Wilmington to participate in a big lawsuit. He called for a bellman to turn off the exit light in the corridor outside his room, which he could see through a transom. The bellman pointed out that he could not do that, since it was against the law and the light was intended for the safety of all the guests. Mr. Darrow snapped,

"Then cover it up, it is annoying me!" The bellman stated he could not do that, either. The night manager was summoned, the same request made, and the same answer given. Mr. Darrow then slammed the door. As the night manager and bellman departed, the manager remarked, "I'll bet that's the first case and appeal that Mr. Darrow has ever lost so quickly."

Someone asks, how do you compare the good old days with today? A number of retirees all start talking. "What good old days? We worked so much harder and so many longer hours than they work today for so much less money. Why, we never knew what benefit plans and unemployment compensation were in those days." All of them did know and understand dependability, quality of service, and dedication to a hotel they all respected.

Finally, as the luncheon comes to an end the retirees, exhausted and all talked out, agree that a sense of humor was necessary for the job. "Hope I am around to see you next year!"

*Watercolor show and sale in the Lobby as part of the annual Christmas Shop*

# Community Awareness

Hotels have a fascinating career. On many occasions, they are the center of activity; their own histories reflect the history of the community they serve. When the Hotel was completed and ready for business, its opening was an event in which the whole city took an interest.

Perhaps the most notable contribution to our community life, in the broad sense, has been in providing and maintaining the Hotel du Pont in the heart of the city. The benefit to the area of the local purchase of supplies is over $2 million annually. Maintenance expenditures, excluding renovations, are $230,000 per year. Taxes are over $400,000 per year, plus $86,000 per year in room sales taxes.

The Hotel's program to draw tour guests from within a 600-mile radius brought 8,000 visitors in 1980 who all spent money on goods and services in our community. Many of these guests return year after year to enjoy Delaware's many cultural and historic attractions.

Within the Du Pont Building in which the Hotel is located are doctors, lawyers, airport transportation, a drugstore, bank, newsstand, haberdasher, realtor, travel agent, jewelry store, brokerage firm, barber shop, tobacco shop, tailor, and laundry.

These are staffed by local employees and businessmen who profit from their trade with the guests. Even a theater is in the same building; the Hotel is one of the few in the country with such a facility, if not the only one.

The Hotel and its staff have provided leadership in many community organizations including the Red Cross, Boy Scouts, Rotary Club, Delaware Hotel-Motel Association, Delaware Restaurant Association, Delaware Travel Council, National Tour Brokers Association, and National Alliance of Businessmen, and in work-study programs by providing instructors and counselors for educational programs. The on-the-job training programs have been of the highest quality. College graduates and students from abroad visit and work as trainees. Scholarships have been arranged with European culinary schools. Many former employees now have their own businesses and others, because of the recognized programs of the Hotel, have obtained jobs and promotions elsewhere in the hotel industry. The great range of civic needs, particularly those requiring volunteers, has been served in many ways by employees of the Hotel du Pont.

These employees, a staff of 490 men and women, have enjoyed continuity of service over the years. Their payroll including benefits exceeds $3 million which makes them the most highly compensated in the country. This standard is important in the areas of quality, dependability, loyalty, concern for the guest, and dignity for the employee himself. Mrs. Eugene Cullum, now eighty-eight years young, an employee from 1916 to 1934, put it well when asked what she would most want to say concerning her years as an employee of the Hotel. "When people plan to attend an affair at the Hotel, it is special, they talk about it, and they are always glad they came. Delawareans are proud of their hotel. I know I am."

The Hotel has been diligent in the field of human relations. Twenty-eight years ago John D. La Mothe, manager of the Hotel, announced at the Walnut Street Y.M.C.A., then a center for the black community, "The Hotel du Pont will not discriminate in accommodating and employment of persons regardless of race, color, or national origin." Bill Frank of the *Morning News* had these comments at the time:

> The news that the Hotel du Pont has an open policy on accommodations, as far as race or national origin is concerned, is the most refreshing thing that has happened in this town in years. A breath of fresh air for Wilmington! I've been a Wilmingtonian long enough to look upon "the hotel" as a gibraltar of respectability and right things. Here in Wilmington, we refer to the Hotel du Pont as "the hotel" in "the building." When you make a date to meet someone in "the hotel," you mean the Hotel du Pont. And for a long time, I thought "the hotel" would be the last in the application of the rule of common decency to people and not on the basis of their race or national origin. If the management of "the hotel" can adopt an open policy, why not other hotels and other eating places? What La Mothe had to say was brief and to the point and without rationalizations or quibbery.[2]

Most important to the Hotel are the respect and pride the citizens take in "their hotel." Almost daily, Wilmingtonians bring their friends to tour the public rooms. It seems to be a highlight for them, a special occasion. The Hotel values this happy relationship and gives serious consideration to the feelings and attitudes of the community when changes are discussed that may have an impact on the public. This cordial and mutual appreciation of one for the other has lasted for nearly seventy years.

Almost from the beginning, in 1920, the interrelationship was pointed out by a Wilmington businessman, David Snellenburg, who had attended the grand opening with a table of ten for dinner. With insight he remarked,

> Some of us in Wilmington who know something about the wonderful Delmarva country want to make Wilmington the window box for the peninsula. To those of us who believe that way and are enthusiastic, the Hotel du Pont is always a suggestion and a demonstration. We see the Hotel du Pont as a hostelry that no other city the size of Wilmington can hope to duplicate and we see the Hotel as part of that window box. That is the reason why we insist on the standard of excellent superiority set by the Hotel du Pont. It is this standard for every exhibit which we will allow in our window box.[3]

[2]"Frankly Speaking," *Wilmington Morning News,* October 16, 1953.
[3]Ernest S. Taite, *Hotel Du Pont* (Wilmington), 1920.

*A painting by Frank G. Tallman, Jr., on display in the Lobby*

# The Art Collection

Through the ages, art has produced an accurate record of man's history, his ideas and ideals, way of life, and mode of dress. In the art galleries of the world can be seen the sum total of man's visual experience, for the artist represents the consciousness and memory of his time.

The arts are important in any city. If the arts are not thriving, something is amiss, because artists are the visionaries, the prophets. They hold a mirror up to us and help us see the difference between things as they are and things as they ought to be. Painters, poets, architects, actors and actresses, musicians: we need them all.

The Hotel du Pont has endeavored to seek out paintings of artistic merit that make a contribution to the cultural life of the community as well as enhance the attractiveness of the Hotel's rooms. The majority are the works of local artists, while others are local in subject matter. These works represent the philosophy of the management, a reflection of the times, and the continuing effort by the Hotel to provide a human interest factor for the enjoyment of guests and visitors. Paintings placed in private and public areas add to the feeling of quality and care and, indeed, to a homelike atmosphere.

The Hotel owns 600 original paintings in several media representing the talents of 214 artists. This body of work is considered to comprise one of the largest and finest collections of its kind in the country. The collection started in the 1940s when the Hotel decided to purchase works by local artists to be used as part of a long range redecoration program. Selection and purchase covered a period of nearly forty years, and the collection now is essentially complete.

The majority of the watercolors were bought from the annual Clothes Line Fair, sponsored by The Studio Group, Inc., and from the annual Christmas Shop. The Studio Group was started in 1935 by several congenial artists who painted together and who later leased and then bought the studios in Wilmington of the late Howard Pyle. In 1964 the Studio Group took charge of the "Artist of the Week" display on the easel in the west end of the Lobby and has shown consistently high standards in its selections. Visitors to the Hotel look forward to the easel painting and have purchased many of the works. The annual Christmas Shop was the first in this country, founded in 1920 by the Women of Trinity Episcopal Church and held since 1924 in the Gold Ballroom. In 1949 it initiated a watercolor show and sale in the Lobby as part of the shop. Other paintings have been bought from the Delaware Arts Festival, held each fall outdoors in Brandywine Park, and from private showings.

In the early stages, these works were framed and were sold on request for the cost involved to a guest or anyone wishing to purchase. This practice was soon discontinued, because it was not the business of the Hotel to buy and sell art works.

Among the artists represented are many of national and international reputation, including Chen Chi; Howard Pyle and several of his students, such as Frank Schoonover; three generations of the Wyeth family, N. C., Andrew, Jamie, and A. N., whose paintings add lustre to the Christina Room, dominated by N. C. Wyeth's *Island Funeral;* area artists such as Carolyn Blish, Edward Loper, Bayard Berndt, Frank Delle Donne,

Charles Colombo, Samuel Homsey, Philip Jamison, John McCoy, Tua Hayes, Edward Grant, and Eugenia Eckford Rhoads, and many others, whose works were bought while they were known only locally and whose reputations now have spread far beyond the area.

Leadership for this venture was provided by Frank G. Tallman, Jr., director of the Du Pont Company's Office Buildings Department, a forward looking gentleman, indeed a visionary. The following observation by Richard P. Sanger best describes Mr. Tallman's and the Hotel's involvement in the collection:

Perhaps no greater encouragement could be given an artist than the assurance that his friends and neighbors are interested in what he is doing—and interested enough to purchase his paintings to decorate their walls. If this is so, artists in the Wilmington area are fortunate.

Along with a brisk community interest in the local artist, a form of patronage which is probably unique and certainly too little recognized has developed in Wilmington. The most responsive local market for the original work of artists from Delaware and neighboring areas of other states has been neither an individual nor an expressly "artistic" institution.

Instead, it has been a hotel—Wilmington's Hotel du Pont, which within the past five years has bought about 200 paintings from area artists and generously donated lobby and window space for exhibits and sales.

The important work of the Hotel du Pont in this field has been quiet and unassuming because of the character of the man who initiated and guided it—the late Frank G. Tallman, Jr. . . . . Mr. Tallman, himself a "Sunday painter," took a keen interest in Delaware painters and in paintings which drew their material from Delaware sources . . . This soft-spoken but fearless critic's advice was frequently sought by friends before they invested in art work for homes and offices.[4]

One sad fact is that Mr. Tallman, the man who did so much to bring it all about, a good artist and fine critic, does not have one of his paintings represented in the collection. Perhaps some day, from a private collection, this gap will be filled.

Another noteworthy comment is the epitaph for Mr. Tallman expressed in 1952 by Dorothy Grafly:

[4] Richard P. Sanger, *Journal-Every Evening* (Wilmington), October 16, 1952.

While it is true that Wilmington art sales are most numerous in the low price range ($1 to $200), the encouragement given the local artist by having his work actually purchased by a fellow townsman cannot be reckoned in dollars and cents, and has led steadily to the development of Delaware art talent. Thus it is not so much the cash art transaction as the feeling of being wanted that gives the artist, whether recognized or incipient, a boost.[5]

The Hotel appreciates the artists' feelings of pride in having their paintings part of this collection. Favorable comments from guests are a great credit to the talent present in each painting and to the Hotel. Hundreds of visitors during the year visit the Hotel to see this collection. Attempts are made to rotate the works as much as possible for the benefit of both the guests and the artists.

[5] Dorothy Grafly, *Art in Focus*, October 1952.

*The Great*
*Formal Rooms*

# Lobby

The Lobby, or residents' area, is known in the hotel industry as the front of the house. For the guests, the Lobby is the arrival and departure area where the console of hospitality is played. The first note can be clearly heard, "Welcome, we thank you for coming." Seventeen other keys must be carefully orchestrated to ensure a memorable visit. The last key, with a soft pedal, sounds, "You honored us by your visit. Please come again."

Let us imagine it is 1930. Most of the guests are delighted by the homelike atmosphere, quiet, and effectiveness of the staff. Talking or noise is not permitted from employees. After 5 p.m. each day, managers wear tuxedos. Guests seated in the Lobby must wear coats. No napping is allowed; the Lobby is not a smoking or reading room but rather the "front door," and those who begin their visits must be favorably impressed. Housekeeping in this area has to be superb at all times.

Bellmen, known in the 1930s as hallmen, escort guests to their rooms. Each day they line up for inspection before each shift and, impeccably dressed, they march to their stations, always facing the guest. Two hallmen are seated on the hallmen's bench to serve as replacements for ones leaving their stations.

Hallmen are unique individuals; they see all, know all, and, we hope, forget all. (Later, these employees would be identified as bellmen because of the little bell at the desk rung to attract their attention. The bell was not accepted well then, nor is it now. Many of these bellmen would be shocked today to see young women serving as bellmen and carrying bags.)

While bellmen room all arriving guests, porters have the responsibility for all departing guests. The Hotel keeps fourteen sample rooms used by companies coming to Wilmington to display their merchandise, always the finest quality, for local merchants. Porters are responsible totally for this activity. (In later years, this particular practice of the bellmen-porters would be discontinued.)

The elevators are sometimes known as cages. Each one has an operator, very professional and pleasant, wearing white gloves. The conversation is limited to, "Good morning," or "Good evening." (No one ever remarked, "Have a nice day.")

Let us now move to the 1950s. "Modern" architecture had a great impact in our country during that decade. The exterior of new buildings would change, making a dramatic difference in the faces of our cities. The interiors also would change; chrome, glass, plastic, and modern designs appeared in furniture, carpets, and accessories. How would this influence affect the Hotel du Pont, which was in need of major renovations? "Let's get the old property up to date." In the Lobby, the main entrance or revolving door located in the center was closed because it was no longer in compliance with city and state safety codes, and two large entrances were created instead. These were stainless steel and glass doors, with a decorative screen of glass separating the new street entrances from the rest of the Lobby. This stark arrangement was softened with a profusion of plants. The beautiful handcrafted furniture, Oriental carpets, and lighting fixtures were replaced with chrome, artificial leather, modern carpets, and new lighting. The handsome reception desk, a highlight of the Lobby, made of walnut and

*Brandywine Village* by A. N. Wyeth

*Master of the Fox Hounds* by Andrew Wyeth

*October Comes* by Frank E. Schoonover

*White House* by Jamie Wyeth

*Island Funeral* by N. C. Wyeth

*Landing in Snow* by Dee Crowley

*Conestoga Powder Wagon* by Howard Pyle

*Skiff in the Cove* by John W. McCoy II

*The Brandywine Room*

The Green Room

*The Christina Room*

*The Gold Ballroom*

Photo by Bob Dickstein
Bill Bard Associates, Inc

set in iron and bronze finished grillwork, was replaced; redesigned and relocated, the desk was covered by plastic with modern grillwork The magnificent ceiling, the walls of travertine, and the floors were kept in place. The Palm Court, so much a part of the Hotel's history, was panelled off with plastic into offices; the mosaic and parquet floors were covered over by a newly designed carpet. The old telephone exchange was removed due to improvements in technology. For guest service, eight telephone booths were installed in the Lobby.

All of these changes had an impact on the exterior of the Hotel. The thirty-seven balconies on the facade along 11th Street were removed. Although not considered architectural gems, they were nevertheless an excellent adaptation of the Italian Renaissance style, but it was reported a number of them had become unsafe. The handsome iron and opal glass marquee, a symbol of elegance for hotels in the early days, was replaced by a new 127 foot-long steel and aluminum marquee which covered the two new entrances.

In September 1958 the local newspaper announced, "Come See the Newly Modernized Hotel du Pont." Such renovations and architecture did not suit all the guests or members of the community. Some were pleased, others were not. However, during this time many positive changes were made. The Hotel was completely air conditioned, bathrooms were modernized, forty-eight guest rooms were added, radios and televisions were installed in the rooms, obsolete elevators were replaced with automatic controls, and in general space was utilized much better.

And now let us return to the present day. How many say, "I'll meet you in the Lobby," or "We'll make our plans in the Lobby." It is a gathering place where friends and families say good-by for the last time, or wait and greet each other in joy and tears. A lonely person enters from the street on a very cold night or very early in the morning and asks, "May I stand here and get warm?" A young person, very upset, comes in and says,

"I ran away from home and am afraid to call the police or my family. Will you help me?" On one occasion, a Marine arrived very late at night with his six month old baby and wanted to know if he could get an inexpensive room. He had come to Wilmington to seek employment. He explained that the baby's mother had died during childbirth, and he declared, "With help, I am going to take care of our child." And so he did.

The Lobby's role as a gathering place has been overplayed at times. In the 1920s, one of the first radios was placed in the Lobby to demonstrate to guests that these newfangled things really worked. The Lobby was filled each evening by people from the street. They would stand quietly to listen to *Amos and Andy,* news broadcasts, and the *Lowell Thomas Show.* Many were heard to say, "Why, it does talk. It's a box with a voice!" The ever-present whiffler, or idle talker (every hotel lobby in the world has one), took it upon himself to explain its workings. No one realized that these boxes with voices in time would include a picture tube: yes, television. Again, the Lobby would be filled by those fascinated in disbelief. Many people came to spend the afternoon and inquired whether chairs were available. Others brought food and snacks. The radio, and later the television, was promptly moved out of the Lobby. From that early beginning, radios and televisions would be installed in all the bedrooms.

The Lobby is also where crowds gather to get a glimpse of a celebrity.

In 1927, the Lobby was filled with guests waiting to see their hero, Charles A. Lindbergh. As he came in, escorted by the late H. B. du Pont, a pioneer in civil aviation, the crowd roared. It was said to be the greatest ovation ever given anyone in the Hotel.

At annual meeting time for the Pepsi-Cola Co. a striking woman entered through the front door. She had beautiful eyes, a face carved from granite, all set off by a large hat. It was Joan Crawford, a director of Pepsi-Cola and the wife of its chairman of the board. Pepsi-Cola was always served during these meetings. On occasion, Miss Crawford thought her Pepsi needed special flavoring which she took care of personally. The maitre d'hôtel put it well, "She was fascinating and gave the meeting such style."

General Douglas MacArthur, chairman of the board, arrived for the Remington Rand board meeting. As he went through the Lobby, even without his famous braided cap and corncob pipe, he walked as though he were on the beaches of the Pacific or the battlefields of Korea. His hair had thinned, and he was not as tall as his photographs would indicate. He was gracious and complimentary, a great American: duty, honor, and country.

During a visit by Bishop Fulton J. Sheen, a newly married couple arrived in the Lobby, and the bishop invited them to his suite and gave them his blessing, an unforgettable experience.

General William Westmoreland had just returned from Viet Nam where he was commander in chief of all forces fighting the Viet Cong. The general, a handsome man, looked every bit the part of a great military leader. He had been invited to address a large gathering in the Gold Ballroom. After the address, the general met the press. He was asked to give his opinion on the Russian presence in Southeast Asia. Quiet and solemn, he answered, "Russia is playing the domino game, one nation after another." The general, now retired and more relaxed, visits Wilmington on occasion. He is always thoughtful in expressing his appreciation for the services provided by the Hotel.

Amelia Earhart came often to visit the Bellanca Aircraft Manufacturing Co. During her last visit to the Hotel, she asked to see her favorite bellman to thank him for all his kindnesses. She placed her hand on his shoulder and said, "I am going to make this flight, and I may never be heard from again." She made the flight and was in fact lost.

Prince Rainier, ruler of the principality of Monaco, arrived escorted by his private chaplain, Father Tucker. The priest had served many years in Wilmington parishes and was loved by many Wilmingtonians. He was quickly surrounded in the Lobby by well-wishers. The prince stood to one side, smiling and amused at being out of the limelight. Father Tucker was embarrassed. The prince had come to this country at Father Tucker's suggestion to meet the parents of actress Grace Kelly, Mr. and Mrs. John B. Kelly of Philadelphia. Some weeks later the engagement was announced, and the beautiful Grace became princess of Monaco.

These anecdotes point out the most fascinating aspect of the Hotel: its guests. Many, of course, have not been from the ranks of the rich and famous, but all who have passed through the Lobby add to its history. If the walls of the Lobby could talk to us, what stories they would tell!

# Green Room

As the guest approaches the Green Room, he enters the foyer, not in place in 1913, through glass doors designed to conform with the same period of ornamentation as the dining room's coffered ceiling. The Lucite panels have been sandblasted in beautiful designs for an edge-lighted effect, and the same ornamental motif has been used on the door handles, cast in bronze. This foyer is now furnished with beautiful antiques, all in keeping with the lovely and gracious Green Room itself, so admired by guests from all over the world. Hanging on the deep green wall to the right is a striking collage of shells, *The White Unicorn*, by Helen Woodring. To the left is the new Green Room Lounge, planned so well that it looks as though it has always been there. It is a delightful place to have a cocktail or to meet a friend before dinner, and it has been described as a classic in good taste by the many ladies who wait for their husbands or guests. The Lounge occupies the space that served as the entrance to the original Lobby and then was leased, in succession, to a ladies' hat shop, an airline reservations service, a jeweler, and a realtor. New also are nearby rest rooms, the lack of which over the years had embarrassed supervision and inconvenienced guests.

Upon entering the dining room, the guest stands quietly, listening to string music coming from the musicians' gallery above. Years ago music was played nightly, but as time passed, this practice was discontinued. Many musicians used to offer to play for no pay; just to perform in the Green Room was reward enough. Still present is the atmosphere of refinement which prevailed during the gala opening nearly seventy years ago.

As the guest admires the fumed oak panelling rising two and a half stories high, his eyes rise to the coffered ceiling now lit with massive chandeliers and sconces purchased in recent years in Spain. The chandeliers weigh 2,500 pounds each. Downlights also have been added. The floor is carpeted with Du Pont Antron III®, which covers the original mosaic and terrazzo floors. In the early history of the Green Room, the beautiful mosaics were covered with Oriental rugs in winter for warmth, and embroidered valances with filet laces of green hung in the windows, reflecting a lovely light upon the marble floors. Today, handsome and rich gold nylon draperies enhance the elegance put in place so many years ago.

As the guest dines, three paintings hanging on the oak panelling add to his pleasure: *Sunflowers,* by Frank E. Schoonover, *Elfreth's Alley,* by Edward L. Loper, and *Garden at Wilmington, Vermont,* by John Koch, all an important part of the Hotel's fine art collection.

On one occasion, a number of men came to the Green Room to discuss its modernization. Even the Swedish Modern style was considered. Looking back now, it is difficult to understand the motivation behind such a proposal for a room that all Wilmingtonians looked upon with pride, that was admired by national and international visitors alike. Among the group were several men who argued in favor of maintaining the purity of the original period. One of them climbed a ladder on the musicians' gallery and washed a small area of the ceiling with soap and water. The dirt that had collected for years disappeared. The entire ceiling was washed, which brought out its original beauty and character, reason prevailed, and the Green Room as we know it was rescued and saved.

The decision to air condition the room was of major importance. While the system was needed, Hotel employees were afraid it would destroy the decor. However, the installation was accomplished subtly and inconspicuously.

The character and personality of this room have always been part of those of its staff. One of these employees, Felix Monferoni, came from Sweden to Wilmington in 1913 at the request of Ernest S. Taite, the first manager of the Hotel. Felix was assigned to the wine cellar to assist Percy Harbison. During Prohibition, he became headwaiter of the Green Room. He was known as a gentleman of the old school and believed in a gracious and formal style of service; he brought great character to the room. Felix left the Hotel to start his own restaurant located nearby on Market Street. After a number of years, he returned to the Hotel to be again headwaiter of the Green Room. He retired in 1948. All of his associates remember him as a professional of the highest order. He is also remembered by the waitresses because he used a cricket which he snapped to gain their attention, a strange procedure for such a quiet man. When this was not acceptable to the waitresses or the guests, the cricket was replaced by the snapping of menus. At the age of seventy-eight he lost his life in an automobile accident a few blocks from the Hotel. He was a great credit to the Hotel, the community, and his family.

The average length of employment for waitresses and their assistants is over twenty-five years; many have served three generations of families. Each one refers to this room as "her" room, as indeed it is. Throughout the Green Room's history, such employees have provided service with dignity, professional concern for the guests, and a high respect for their own performances.

Because of their long service, the waitresses have had all

kinds of experiences with the guests. The late John L. Lewis, president of the United Mine Workers, came to the Hotel many times. His favorite was the Green Room. He ate alone and always ordered lamb chops for lunch or dinner. The only comment he ever made was, "These are the best prepared lamb chops in the country." The waitresses thought he stopped in Wilmington just to have his lamb chops.

Connie Mack, the owner and manager of the Philadelphia Athletics, often stayed at the Hotel and enjoyed dining in the Green Room. He also ate alone, never checking the famous straw hat he used to move his players around during a game. The hat was as much a part of his personality as the high starched collar he wore. After dinner, he would carefully audit his check and then with great precision lift the plate and place ten cents under it. The waitresses watched this exercise with great interest and were heard to say, "If Mr. Mack manages his baseball club with as much precision as he tips, then no wonder they win pennants!" It was their judgment that he paid his players more generously than he tipped.

For a number of years one waitress had been serving a couple who regularly had dinner in the Green Room. Once, with the room nearly filled, the lady stood up to leave, and a delicate undergarment dropped around her feet. Without the slightest hesitation, she stepped out of the garment and her husband picked it up and put it in his pocket. The waitress said, "I have never seen such an embarrassing moment handled so beautifully, but it must have happened before."

A guest of the Green Room arrived each Sunday for dinner and asked to be seated near the door. The waitresses called her Gravel Gertie among themselves. She would interrupt her dinner and leave to return to her chauffeured limousine to hear the broadcast of the *Edgar Bergen Show* and Charlie McCarthy.

Two guests who had been served regularly by a waitress for a number of years learned she had been widowed and left with four children. In a few days, she received a letter stating that they would assume the cost of her children's education. In recalling this, the waitress said, "None of my children took advantage of that offer, but it was a memory that will be with me the rest of my life."

A similar tragedy happened to another waitress with a large family. When her predicament became known among the guests, generous amounts of money were given, some anonymously and others directly, to help her through that trying time. This is guest relations at its finest.

It would be rare for any dignitary visiting Wilmington not to dine in the Green Room. During a week's time, you might see Philippe Cousteau at lunch while his father Jacques met with Du Pont Company officials about a television program. This handsome young man would lose his life in a plane crash. At a nearby table would be Jane Goodall, the anthropologist, quietly having lunch (quite a contrast to living with apes in the jungle). Gene Autry and his wife also dined in the Green Room, and some say he was interested in purchasing the Hotel. The real purpose of his visit was to see the Hotel du Pont since he had heard so much about it. Two or three times a year James Farley would entertain guests, and among his favorites was Mrs. Franklin D. Roosevelt. On one occasion, he arranged for her to receive the check. She was startled for a moment, and he laughed with delight; this was a favorite joke of his. Mrs. Roosevelt paid it. One very special affair in the Green Room involved the three astronauts, who had just returned from their trip to the moon.

It was always a rare moment when all three brothers, Pierre, Lammot, and Irénée du Pont, came for lunch. On one occasion, Mrs. R. R. M. Carpenter, their sister, was already in the Green Room having lunch with friends. A general silence fell over the entire room. To be seated now at the table once reserved for Mr. Pierre is very special.

During lunch one day, Rosalind Russell entered the room

and received a spontaneous standing ovation for her performance in *Auntie Mame*. The actress was deeply moved. This
ovation was the first and only one ever given in the Green
Room.

The president of Continental American Life Insurance Co.
often is seated at the corner table on the 11th and Market
Streets side. That corner might have been his office. Not many
people know that, during 1910, the insurance company constructed its first executive office building on this same site.
The building was never occupied by Continental American, because it was purchased by the Du Pont Company for its own
office complex which would include the Hotel du Pont. Associations between the insurance company and the Hotel have
been warm and cordial all through the years.

Let us quote three of the many letters that best describe the
feelings of guests. Dr. John H. Jenny of Wilmington wrote, "We
had just been married and drove to Wilmington to have lunch
in the Green Room. We were captured by the beauty and formality of the room. That was in August 1940. Little did we
realize Wilmington would become our home in 1951. Over the
years, we would arrange and attend many affairs in the Hotel
du Pont. The most meaningful was a party given for my retirement in the Gold Ballroom. A few weeks ago, our children called
and asked us for dinner in the Green Room for our fortieth
anniversary. A memorable affair for my wife and me and, I
hope, for the Hotel." Indeed it was, and we thank you. W. A.
Stanton, the retired export manager of the Du Pont Company's
Photo Products Department, reported, "Just recently, three Co-
lombians were here for almost a week. I did not see them until
their last day. When we sat down for lunch in the Green Room,
one of them said, 'This is the fifth meal we have had here.' I
said, 'I'm very sorry, we should have taken you out some place.'
Their leader replied, 'Oh, no, this is one of the best restaurants
that we know in the United States.' " Robert L. Richards, executive vice president of the American Hotel & Motel Associa-

tion, considers the Hotel du Pont one of the outstanding hotels in America, a great credit to the hospitality industry. "The Hotel du Pont has a richness such as no other hotel I have ever visited. It's a mixture of infinite delicacy and grandeur, much like the finest properties in Europe, with a distinct American flavor of 'home.' The marvelous artwork tastefully decorating the walls, the chandeliers from Europe in the main dining room, the beautiful decor of the ballroom, and the welcome smile for all visitors leave nothing more to be desired. Each visit has been a rare opportunity to ooh and ah for hours and later to think how nice my next visit will be . . . I can hardly wait."

A lady eighty years young was asked by her grandchildren what she would like most for a birthday celebration. After a pause, she answered, "I've lived in Wilmington all my life, and I have never eaten in the Green Room. I would like that most."

# Brandywine Room

During the opening of the Hotel in 1913, the area now known as the Brandywine Room then was identified as a walnut panelled writing room or hallway, often referred to as Peacock Alley. It was used as an entryway to the Club Room.

In 1941 the Brandywine Room opened as a luxurious cocktail lounge and rendezvous for informal buffet luncheons and dinners. It occupied the space of the former brokerage offices, the writing room, the Hotel manager's office, and the telephone exchange. At the entrance were two huge, handcarved mahogany doors which once graced a palatial home on Fifth Avenue in New York. The room was panelled in rich old American walnut, lit by hammered iron bracket lamps taken from other areas of the Hotel. The bar was made from a single piece of mahogany twenty-six feet long. The walls were decorated with a number of pictures loaned by the Du Pont Company museum: hunting scenes, Du Pont powder barrels, a naval battle painted in the early 1800s, old maps, engravings showing the battle between the *Java* and the *Constitution,* the engagement between the *Monitor* and the *Merrimac.* Such scenes created a sense of history and reflections of our country's early beginnings and added an aura of coziness, comfort, and warmth.

The room has changed very little over the years. It is considered an informal room, restful, a meeting place. Little change has taken place in its decor. The beautiful mahogany doors now have been replaced by Lucite to conform to the architecture of the building corridor. The walnut panelling now is enhanced by many beautiful and well-known paintings from the Hotel's own collection of fine art.

This room, over the years, has served many guests in many different ways. It is a meeting place for the great Broadway producers and stars. Some come to enjoy a cocktail, others to confess and talk at the bar, enjoy lunch or dinner (either social or business), some to be seen, others not to be seen, and yes, some who prefer to be alone. In most cities this room would be known as a smart and sophisticated lunch and dinner place.

Vincent Price, the actor, gourmet, and art critic, was entertaining Gregory Peck and others in the Brandywine Room. He invited his guests to see the Wyeth art collection in the adjoining Christina Room. As he departed, he advised the headwaiter that he was expecting a lady to join them and to please escort her to the Christina Room. As the lady entered the Brandywine Room, the headwaiter realized that she was the great actress Helen Hayes, who had just starred in the movie *Airport*. An excited woman approached Miss Hayes and exclaimed, "You are from the airport!" Everyone laughed as the embarrassed woman sat down, still unable to remember the actress's name.

Don Ameche appeared in a number of shows at the Playhouse. During each visit, he asked the manager of the dining room to sit with him and go over every minute detail of the preparation and service of his dinner. While the manager thought this attention not necessary, Mr. Ameche did have a great knowledge of food and its preparation.

At 4 p.m. Ingrid Bergman might enter the room with her two attractive daughters, Isabella and Ingrid Rossellini, and sit in a booth for nearly an hour, quietly talking and drinking tea and coffee. Miss Bergman, still a beautiful woman, seems to enjoy her privacy at this moment. Four o'clock is the favorite time for many of the stars appearing at the Playhouse to gather in the Brandywine Room. Most of the producers, directors, and performing artists have dinner in this room after the show.

Behind the great mahogany bar are three bartenders representing an average of over thirty-five years of service: Paul Caldwell, Mike Mazick, and Joe Bannon. Each one is a legend, with his own sense of humor and a marvelous ability to listen and discuss any subject with great expertise. As Joe put it, "We are diversified in our knowledge, and to think we share it freely with the guest without an appointment. I think we have been helpful to many guests who have passed our way."

In fact, one time a gentleman entered the Brandywine Room and asked to be seated at the bar. He appeared badly crippled and walked with difficulty on crutches. A little later, after three or four drinks, the gentleman walked out without his crutches. The mystery is that the bartender, to this day, is unable to remember the content of the drinks. This loss is sad, because whatever it was produced a quick and lasting cure.

# Christina Room

In 1913 this classic and superbly planned room was named the Club Room. For years it was used for reading or relaxing, occasional afternoon teas or special dinners to honor visiting dignitaries. The handcarving in delicate detail on the imported walnut walls is superb; its equal is not found any other place in the Hotel. This room was Pierre S. du Pont's favorite, and no other area more clearly set forth his character and personality. We will not repeat the story of the handcarving, the three skylights or the great batik tapestry. Much of the cost of these items was assumed by Mr. du Pont.

The main entrance to this room was from what is now known as the Lobby. As the guest entered, he passed by a checkroom set like a picture in a lovely handcarved walnut frame. Guests often stopped in silence to admire it. Furnishings were changed a number of times, always suited to the proportion and scale of the elegant architecture. In those days, the decorations were as Mr. du Pont would have them.

As time moved forward, the need for additional dining facilities in the Hotel increased. But problems for food service in this room were present, especially noise and the lack of a food preparation kitchen. All new recommendations would have largely destroyed the decor. Finally, time would take its toll, and the three skylights would be removed after a report that they had become unsafe. One was found to have been installed upside down. The batik tapestry, *A Legend of Hospitality,* was taken down from the imported roseal marble fireplace.[1] During the changes, the entrance from the Lobby was closed for a number of years.

Because of its beauty and excellent location, the need to serve the Hotel and improve utilization of space, reevaluations would go forward. After careful studies, it was decided that the scheme of the room would be largely maintained. In 1964 the name would be changed from the Club Room to the Christina Room. The plans were to use the Brandywine and Christina Rooms individually and together, just as these two rivers flow separately and together in Wilmington. The pantry would be enlarged, the ceiling lowered for noise control, and lighting and air conditioning improved. A foyer again would open into the Lobby. Custom made furniture would be obtained, and the finest crystal would grace the tables. On the great walnut-panelled walls would hang some of the most famous paintings from the Hotel's collection. Today, it is a small but elegant museum of Wyeth family works. Hundreds of guests and visitors come each year to enjoy these paintings, and the guests who dine nightly always are pleased by the display of art and the comfort of the room.

These two rooms enjoy a national and international reputation for fine dining. While both rooms are used together, each still maintains its own charm, character, beauty, and individuality.

During the opening of the refurbished Christina Room, a young captain joined the Hotel staff and was placed in charge of this room. He was a highly trained professional with all the certificates qualifying him for cookery at tableside. During the evening, the manager of the Hotel arrived with guests. Knowing

[1] It is still a mystery as to what happened to this priceless item, the missing piece of a great collection on exhibit in the Metropolitan Museum of Art in New York.

the captain's skill in table cookery, he asked him to prepare crêpes Suzette. He burned the crêpes. No greater embarrassment could happen to a professional, particularly at the manager's dinner. Forgiveness is wonderful. The young man now manages one of the finest hotels in the country.

# Du Barry Room and Gold Ballroom Suite

To enter the Gold Ballroom suite from the Lobby, the guest passes through two twelve-foot high American walnut doors handcarved with designs of peacocks and urns. These doors are set in a frame of Italian roseal marble, carved to look like basket weaving. At the top is massive handcarved Caen stone imported from France. The guest truly is prepared for a grand entrance.

Beyond the doors, he pauses to see part of the whole suite of rooms opened in 1919 to replace the smaller original ballroom, which had been located on the eleventh floor in 1912. Above him now is the ornate Italian coffered ceiling executed in gold leaf. To visit the du Barry Room, he climbs the elaborate roseal marble staircase set off by a balustrade of polished steel and bronze. The walls of the hall are of travertine stone, imported from Italy and soft and warm in color.

As he enters the du Barry Room, the guest is taken past three doorways also of handcarved American walnut. The ceiling is low in contrast to the many high ceilings one finds elsewhere in the Hotel, because the room is located at the end of the mezzanine directly above the Ballroom. White pillars, old rose hangings, and parquet floors give the room a splendid character of its own. During recent renovations, its beauty was enhanced by the installation of a magnificent crystal chandelier and wall sconces. The crystal was imported from Yugoslavia through Austria, and the fixtures were then custom made in New York by Metropolitan Lighting. At the end of the room are three large mirrored doors which can be opened for guests to enjoy the festivities below in the Ballroom, as they look down from balconies edged with handcrafted bronze railings.

Architecturally, the du Barry Room is of the Empire or Federal period. During the last quarter of the eighteenth century, inspired by discoveries at Pompeii, ancient Roman art began to reexert its influence on architecture and interior design. Many of these motifs were developed to reinforce the imperial glory of Napoleon I of France and resulted in that phase of decoration known as the Empire style. At the same time in the United States, this style, slightly modified and lightened, was termed Federal.

As the guest leaves the du Barry Room and descends the stairs, he now enters the reception area, or social entrance to the Ballroom. This small room has its own personality and purpose, with a low ceiling, travertine walls, and Tennessee marble floor. This room also may be entered from 11th Street, a private entrance often used with a canopy for special social events. It is sparsely furnished because it functions as a gathering place and, more often than not, it is used by Hotel supervision who greet and direct the guest to the check room and lounges below.

The guest now is welcomed by the host and hostess who are standing in the foyer of the Gold Ballroom. He walks down the marble steps to greet them, onto a polished parquet floor partly covered by three matching Oriental carpets. The furnishings are eighteenth century French in style. The walls are panelled and painted in old ivory highlighted with gold. On the right wall are three elegant glass panels that reflect the neoclassic period in garlands, festoons, swags, and wreaths composed of flowers and fruit, tied by a ribbon bowknot with flowing ends.

On the left wall are two paintings depicting pastoral scenes by Francesco Zuccarelli (1702–1788) and the painting, *Venetian Courtyard,* by M. K. Franeschi.

All of the guests have been welcomed and introduced. The hostess now turns to the supervisory headwaiter who always keeps in eye contact with her. She smiles, raises her hand, and the doors of the Ballroom are opened, the gold draperies are drawn. The excitement and expectations of the guests are fulfilled.

This magnificent room is one of the most beautiful ballrooms in the world. The decoration of the room is dedicated to love. Above the highly polished oak floor in the motifs of the ceiling border of great gilt and blue rosettes are Columbines and Pierrots, little comic characters from old French pantomime, who wink and nod and say, "This is our room, we will watch over you and be a happy part of your visit." The undecorated panel in the ceiling is typical of the neoclassic or Louis XVI style. From it hang two large handcarved wooden French chandeliers, attached to elaborate rosettes.

Supported by allegorical figures in the spandrels are medallions of twenty beautiful women: the Queen of Sheba, Delilah, Helen of Troy, Dido, Cleopatra, Agrippina, Theodosia, Guinevere, Florinda, Scheherazade, Beatrice D'Este, Vespucci,[2] Mary Stuart, Pocahontas, Catherine of Russia, Madame du Barry, Lady Hamilton, Theodosia Burr, Josephine of France, and Tis-An, Empress of China. These ladies made history; indeed, they changed history.

The walls are executed in sgraffito, a kind of scratching dating from the Italian Renaissance. The process consists of multiple layers (usually five) of colored plaster, in which the design is handcut or scratched with special tools; the depth of the cut or scratch determines the color of the design. Thirty Italian artisans were imported to execute this decoration, which re-

[2] The medallion indeed reads Vespucci, which might be a misspelling of Vespasia. It is likely that Theodosia is an error for the Empress Theodora and Tis-An an error for Tzu-Hsi.

quired over one year of work; it now is a lost art. The personalities of these great craftsmen can be detected in each panel. The principal mural figures depict colorfully costumed dancing girls of various nationalities, interspersed with draped mythological figures of classical origin.

Large mirrors around the room are framed with Corinthian columns. The base of each frame is decorated with a ram's head, and the top with bees, surmounted by an urn (typical of the Louis XVI period). The mirrors have been slanted slightly so that the dancers may see themselves as they waltz.

The story of love begins with the first of four oval figures, or cartouches, located over doors at each corner of the Ballroom. These depict the courtship of birds, fishes, and stars and reveal the humor of the early twentieth century artisans. In the first cartouche at the top are two doves resting quietly in a sunburst (representing a new day). Next, two little cupids are kneeling, one holding an urn of grapes (food and wine), and the other a tambourine (gaiety). The final scene is the moon and stars; all is very quiet, and the moon is just peeking through the clouds.

At the springing line, we encounter octagonal plaques which depict Beauty and Strength, holding roses; Fortune and Luxury, with a wheel of fortune; Love and Romance, holding a loving cup; and Fame and Power, or majesty, with a crown.

The story begins to unfold. In the second cartouche, the doves are awake and have moved closer together. The two cupids are beginning to move, the moon has started to rise, and fishes are swimming about in glee. In the third cartouche, the doves are looking at each other in a very positive manner. The moon is rising rapidly, the little cupids are offering grapes and shaking the tambourine, and lovebirds are close together on their branch. By the fourth cartouche, the moon is full and laughing, the cupids are happy, and salamanders are making love. As the guest again looks at the ceiling, the little Pierrots are smiling their approval.

Gold draperies are hung at each tall arched window in the room. In each corner, very near the ceiling, is the monogram

DH. The architects became so engrossed in the greatness of the room that they wished to give it its own special identity.

This room has witnessed moments of heartache and tears. Let us suppose it is Saturday afternoon, and the wedding ceremony has been completed. The bride and groom arrive at the Hotel for their reception in the Gold Ballroom, an event planned for so long, the most important in their young lives. Following are the mother and father of the bride. They are not happy and think, "Why him, she had many chances to do much better." The mother and father of the groom have similar thoughts in reverse. As the receiving line forms in the foyer, the guests begin to feel the tension. Secretly, the bride sheds a tear. No one smiles in the receiving line.

Then the doors of the Ballroom are opened, and the gold draperies are drawn. As the guests enter, the orchestra is playing softly, but the little Pierrots are disturbed and shake their heads; they are not happy. As the reception moves forward, it is time for the duty dances. When the parents dance together, they begin to feel the majesty of the room, the atmosphere of the occasion. Their thoughts run, "After all, this is not our wedding, and we have not acted as we should. It is theirs."

The change is immediately felt throughout the reception. The little Pierrots smile and wink with pleasure, the moon laughs and nods. Most importantly, the bride and groom are engulfed in happiness and forgiveness. Love is in place; yes, with the holding of the roses, beauty and strength; with the loving cup, now held by the bride and groom, love and romance; the wheel of fortune has turned; and the couple are crowned with majesty. They will live happily ever after.

The Culinary Arts

# The Food Operation

The Hotel du Pont administers the largest food operation in the world for a hotel of its size. During the year, 1,306,000 guests are served (excluding the vending operation), representing a sales volume of $8,580,000. This is a very large and complex responsibility. What is required to manage effectively an operation of this magnitude?

The primary objective for all services provided by the Hotel was set forth during a meeting of the founders in 1911: "the highest quality—no compromise." To obtain this objective, seven basics were established: specifications must be developed for all items; all items must be purchased and received according to those specifications; storage and refrigeration must be effective; items first in must be requisitioned first out; the food must be prepared by the finest chefs; the food must be served by professionals in the most attractive surroundings; and for implementation, each of these basics must have established controls and follow-up, individually and collectively.

How is it possible to implement the primary objective, the highest quality, in such a diversified operation? Through the organization, the staff, and the administration.

The Food and Beverage manager has the responsibility for

the total operation, divided into five carefully defined production and service areas, each with its own manager with complete autonomy. These areas are Food Preparation, which provides food preparation and service for the sales outlets, Dining Rooms, Banquet, Cafeterias and Nemours Soda Shop, and Vending. The managers of these operations comprise the staff of the general manager. Each area is identified as a profit center and could be discontinued without affecting the other operations. Satisfactory financial results are expected and are necessary in any successful business.

To staff the Food and Beverage operation requires 370 employees. Of these, the central preparation area, or kitchen, alone requires 119 persons. The executive chef assigns a chef and his staff to each sales outlet. This arrangement enables the manager of these operations to have, in effect, his own preparation team, necessary for communication, menu planning, availability of food, cost, serving times, schedule, and staffing. It in no way interferes with flexibility or backup from the central kitchen. All food preparation personnel report to the executive chef. Satellite operations such as the three cafeterias, Nemours Soda Shop, and Vending require a staff of ninety-one employees; this means a total of 210 employees are directly involved in the preparation and serving of food. The sales areas, such as Banquet and Dining Rooms, employ a staff of 160. These employees include sales staff, headwaiters, and waitresses.

The manager of the Hotel meets each morning with his staff to discuss the details involved in the previous day's performance. This is known as fine tuning. At the same meeting, the present day's activities are discussed, and all areas of responsibility assigned. Weekly, a complete review is made of each sales operation and is attended by the managers of the areas, the Food and Beverage manager, and the general manager. Monthly, the cost information arrives, the moment of truth. Much time is given to preparing information for the forecasts, which are required each year for safety, food sanitation, training, and employee relations. Most important is how these forecasts will be attained. The results of this meeting then are reviewed with the director of the General Services Department. Cross-examination is sometimes very direct and difficult, particularly if the forecast has not been met. Yearly, the highest level of management in the Du Pont Company reviews and discusses the Hotel's performance, indeed its very reason for being. This interview is truly an experience for the Hotel administration.

# The Chefs

Why were good professional chefs and cooks so few in early America? Because native Americans did not look upon cookery as a profession. For many years, people involved in the preparation and serving of food in this country were considered and classified as servants. This attitude was embarrassing and unacceptable to European chefs and maitres d'hôtel.

The first chefs and cooks that came to this country kept the secrets of their trade to themselves. Great hotels and restaurants brought their chefs from France, Switzerland, Germany, Austria, and Italy. Each chef brought with him his own crew, employing other kitchen help from his own national background.

During the opening of the Hotel du Pont, and even today to some degree, this policy was followed. The first executive chef, E. Garraux, came from the Gotham Hotel in New York with twenty food preparation experts. The staff was completed with other key employees from other cities. Shortly after his arrival, Mr. Garraux became displeased with a regulation he received from management and proceeded to walk out, taking with him his production chefs. Management was able to employ a number of well-known black cooks from the Wilmington area to continue food service. The next morning, the executive chef returned with threats. Protection had been provided for the cooks, and no conflict developed, but this action troubled one of the Hotel's founders, Pierre S. du Pont. Plans were put in place to prevent such actions in the future.

In 1930–31, a similar action occurred. However, on this occasion, all the employees who walked out were terminated. Food preparation professionals still remember friends and the days of teams, but this arrangement now has largely disappeared.

What is life like in a kitchen administered by professional chefs of long and hard experience? The acceptance of an executive chef in a kitchen is not easy for him or his associates. The kitchen is the chef's domain. He will hear from the employees, "Do you think you own this place?" The chef, "No, but I feel I do." These chefs are proud, sensitive, artistic, impatient, perfectionistic, high-strung, short-fused, and dedicated to hard work. They are kind to those who wish to learn the art of cookery, brutal yet forgiving to those who have no respect for quality. Many of them are walking recipe books, yet all have their own collections of reference material which are used often. Their ability in planning great affairs is most satisfying to them. All great chefs continually are seeking an assignment that will challenge their years of training. To become an outstanding chef usually requires twenty years of training, much of it gained by serving under great chefs in different parts of the world for little compensation or, in some cases, for none at all. As a chef stands at the range with his pots and pans and the items he is preparing, the expression on his face as he cooks and tastes will reveal at once whether the dish is a success or a failure.

One of the most prized possessions of a chef is his fine collection of cutlery, exceeding a cost of $1,000. It would be rare indeed for a chef to loan anyone this equipment. The knife sharpener, who arrives weekly, is honored if the chef permits him to sharpen his knives.

You may ask, why the tall hat or the handkerchief around the neck? Centuries ago throughout Europe, chefs were considered by rulers of nations as the most important members of their households. An attempt to entice a chef to leave his job could cause a serious diplomatic confrontation. From time to time, wars rolled back and forth across Europe. To protect the chefs who were high on the list for capture by the invaders, they were hidden in monasteries and dressed in the garb of dignitaries of the Church. The tall hats were worn as a disguise. The chefs were grateful for such protection and have continued to wear the high white hat to this day. The handkerchief worn around the neck is a formal part of the dress code. It is also helpful since temperatures in the kitchen may reach 85–100°F during food preparation.

To better understand a chef's personality and character, the executive chef of the Hotel du Pont, Hubert M. Winkler, was interviewed. A challenge to any chef's professional background is the administration of a very large, complex, and diversified food operation where quality and portion controls are primary. At the Hotel du Pont, his is a prestigious and unique position: unique to be employed in such a post by the Du Pont Company, the largest chemical company in the world; to be required to follow procedures such as safety, food sanitation, and programs affecting employee relations established many years ago.

Q. Chef, how do you rate the culinary arts training programs in America today with those in Europe?

A. America has made great progress in this area of training. In most programs, they are comparable to those in Europe. The Hotel du Pont is an example of what can be accomplished. The training over the years has been so meaningful that today we have many employees, men and women, in positions of great responsibility. For example, two summer trainees, graduates of the Culinary Institute, have been accredited scholarships in one of Switzerland's most prestigious schools. The real breakthrough is the fact that one is female. This would have been unheard of a few years ago. (The chef did not say that his efforts and contacts in that school were most helpful.)

Q. What is your background, Chef?

A. I am an Austrian. I attended school in my native country and specialized in the basics of the culinary arts. Upon graduation, after four years, I obtained a job in Switzerland to begin advanced training for seven more years. From this experience, I would become known in the world of cookery as "Swiss trained." I then travelled to many countries, including France, Germany, Bermuda, and back to Switzerland for the purpose of improving my knowledge in specific areas of food preparation. During these many stops, I became proficient in languages.

The chefs I worked for were internationally known. Some of the chefs were helpful, others were not. I might receive a minimum of pay or nothing. The hours were unbelievable. In one location, I did not see the sun for two months, since the shift was from 4 a.m. until 10 p.m. A high price to pay, but I learned.

I joined the Hotel du Pont as an area chef in 1973. In 1974, I was promoted to executive chef.

Two areas of responsibility and knowledge for a chef to learn and never forget are the butcher shop and pilferage. A butcher shop makes or breaks an executive chef. It receives more attention than any other part of the operation. Pilferage is always in place; it does not go away. It occurs in every hotel in the world. It can and must be controlled. The Hotel du Pont has many audits and sophisticated procedures to deal with this problem. The most important control is that the majority of the employees are honest and will not tolerate a shadow of dishonesty to be cast over their employment.

Even more serious and difficult to control is pilferage by guests. Pilferage costs hotels around the world enormous amounts of money each year. Some guests think they are only souvenir gathering. But when guests remove linen, china, glass, silver, and other items of value without paying for them, they are clearly stealing. Why do guests attempt to justify such action with the comment, "it is just a souvenir"? If any guest invited to your house took home a spoon or a towel, what would be your reaction? Is there a difference? The Hotel does not think so.

When an employee is found leaving the Hotel's premises without a removal permit for an item, he is subject to termination. Yet the guests take these items without hesitation. The Hotel du Pont is happy to sell souvenirs to guests who want them and has set up a remembrance cabinet displaying items that may be purchased. Many guests take advantage of this service.

But I've interrupted my story. As I moved on, I began to fully appreciate the meaning of professionalism and developed a sense of pride for all that the culinary arts stand for. My commitment would have other effects on my life. I would work long hours and have a sense of pride and acceptance of full responsibility for all food preparation. For the first time, it dawned on me that my hours of work would be determined by the guests. My social life, if indeed I have any, would become lonely. My work seemed to take priority over all. Not many wives would understand that devotion. It is not fair to ask anyone else to accept my personal commitment.

Q. May we ask how other professionals like you find time for a social life?

A. In many cases, they marry someone they have worked with who understands such work schedules.

Q. You may have answered the question, Chef, there is someone out there! How many employees are required to assist you in such a large and diversified operation?

A. I am assisted by nine chefs, sixteen cooks, five cook assistants, ten pantry service helpers, fifteen commissary employees, five storeroom receivers, thirteen bakers, and thirty stewards. (These exclude the cafeterias, Nemours Soda Shop, and Vending).

Q. While you are not responsible for the sales and food service, your operation does have a direct impact on it. How many employees are needed in this area?

A. Eleven headwaiters and captains, eighty waitresses and

assistants, and fifteen bartenders. (These exclude cleaning employees).

Q. What do you as chef enjoy most?

A. An excellent staff that demonstrates by its performance that it cares; menu planning and the execution of those menus; being a part of employee development; drawing up specifications for all food purchased; and maintaining the forecast for all labor and food costs.

Q. When you mention menu planning, what is actually required?

A. First, sales history, and a knowledge of the guests through input from the dining rooms; then, the equipment and facilities necessary to prepare all the foods set forth on the menu. Portion control is most important. For example, the law requires that variances in the cutting of steaks cannot be more than one-quarter ounce. I cannot overemphasize the importance of truth in the menu. And menus now must show flexibility, since travel by ladies has increased greatly as has international travel. I always consider what foods are available locally, since our area is well known for its vegetables, seafood, and poultry.

Q. What are the different types of food service and which does the Hotel du Pont primarily use?

A. Many countries around the world provide food service in keeping with their cultural backgrounds. All food service has been refined over the centuries, with variations brought about by social changes and the accessibility of equipment.

Russian service is identified improperly in America as French service. It first appeared widely in Europe during the Napoleonic Wars. Because of its simplicity and speed, it has become the most accepted service in fine restaurants. The food is prepared and precut in the kitchen and then arranged by the chef on silver platters. The guest is served from these platters.

English food is presented to the guest in large pieces, such as a roast of beef, from the kitchen. It may be cut at the guest's table or removed to a side table for preparation and serving. Today, this type of service largely has been discontinued.

French service, for a great many years, was recognized as the ultimate and was used extensively throughout Europe. Heating and garnishing of food are conducted at the side table, or guéridon.

American food is plated in the kitchen and placed before the diner. The food can be served quickly, and side support dishes are used in this type of service.

The Hotel du Pont's food service is primarily American in the public dining rooms and for large private functions. However, for smaller private affairs, any service requested by the guest can be provided. A combination of Russian and French service can be used effectively with American service. The Hotel has the equipment and trained employees to utilize any one of the four services.

Q. Employment records show that from 1947 to 1950 many dieticians were employed for the kitchen operation. Would you comment?

A. Yes. This was the period after World War II, and continental chefs were not available. In fact, very few chefs of quality were available in this country. The dieticians, while trained for institutional feeding, were assigned to the preparation areas to improve food quality and production. From all I've learned, this action proved effective. Today, two of those dieticians are in supervisory positions. In my judgment, the flexibility needed in menu planning and preparation would not lend itself to the most effective use of these professionals.

Q. What is your feeling concerning the use of frozen foods, or convenience foods?

A. From 1959 to 1962 the Hotel du Pont embarked on an ambitious program to determine the use of such foods. The motivation for this study was to control labor costs, food cost or portion control, and increase menu choices. After an in-depth study, the use of such foods was placed in abeyance. Three important areas needed more study: research to better prepare, package, and store the foods and equipment for reconstituting;

education for employees in handling such foods; and broad communications to examine the total concept. It is most difficult to convince a professional chef that you can freeze food, then reconstitute it, and not lose flavor. Also, you tend to have one food quality; you feel locked in, or as one chef put in, "frozen in." A diversified food operation would have difficulty with it. Today, frozen foods, or convenience foods, are not used to any extent in the Hotel du Pont.

Because of the importance of this subject, I might call your attention to a recommendation made by a supervisor during the development of the tour business. The recommendation set forth many reasons why frozen foods should be considered for the tour guests. More studies were made to determine the feasibility of such a recommendation. It was rejected. As you know, the tour business has grown to be very important in the sales mix. The tour brokers report that the most favorable comments they receive from these guests concern the excellent quality of the food served by the Hotel.

Q. What happens to leftover foods?

A. In the early days, children from St. Joseph's Home for Boys would come for the food to be used in the institution. Today, with few exceptions, it is discarded.

Q. What are a chef's most difficult problems?

A. I have found them to be these: having European chefs understand safety and food sanitation; giving oral presentations to large groups; communicating with each food preparation area, or what is known in the culinary arts as "one language"; dealing with the paper work for employee relations; deciding who comes first: management or the guest; coping with pilferage, which must receive major attention.

Q. What is the monthly use of wines and brandies in Hotel cookery?

A. Twelve different wines and brandies of quality are used representing 3,700 bottles per month.

The executive chef continued with the following comments:

We are proud of our accomplishments in the conservation of energy. During the opening of the Hotel, coal and gas were used and now only electricity and steam. Gas is the choice of most chefs. It provides instant heat, it is hotter, low in cost, and maintenance free. On the other hand, gas uses a great deal of oxygen in a kitchen, and it is not advisable to keep it on in a small area for a long period of time.

The food preparation facilities accommodate 8,000 guests per day and average 3,500 meals per day, and on some days, 5,000. The weather causes a dramatic swing in food preparation. For example, on rainy days the Hotel guests and Du Pont Company employees stay to eat within the buildings.

The stewards in the dish area wash 14,000 pieces of china per day. Many guests fail to realize that should this not take place, we would have no food service. The stewards responsible for the pots and pans clean 200 items per day. Again, no pots, no cookery.

Employees' meals in the Hotel are the finest in the country. Most foods are the same as those the guest receives.

# A Gourmet Dinner

Gastronomy is the art of good eating.
A gourmet is a connoisseur of food and beverage.
A gourmand is one who is excessively fond of eating and drinking.

All too often, gourmet dinners are misunderstood. Some would-be guests think that the dinners are overpriced; they could not possibly eat all that food or drink all that wine; they would not know which fork or wine glass to use; they would not be able to identify many of the courses. A gourmet dinner is not just eating out. It is a total experience, an evening always to remember. The guests will not be gorged with food and wine, and the evening will go by surprisingly fast. The concern for cost will no longer matter.

There are not many restaurants that serve gourmet food and wine on a regular basis. Such restaurants are usually small and seat twenty or thirty guests. While a number of restaurants serve outstanding food, few are identified as truly gourmet establishments.

The planning of a gourmet dinner is the highest responsibility any chef can assume. His first decision is to decide the theme and number of courses, usually eight to twelve. At this point, all of his long training and expertise come into play; his repu-

# Soirée Gastronomique

### Mignardises
*Champagne Piper Heidsieck Magnum Brut 1973*

### Parfait de Langouste
*Muscadet de Sèvres et Maine Loire 1976*
*Domaine de la Bâtardière*

### Consommé Viveur

### Pain de Saumon à la Valoise
Sauce Foyot
*Meursault Les Charmes 1977*

### Suprêmes de Faisan aux Beaux-Fruits
*Château Talbot Grand Cru Classé Médoc Magnum 1970*

### Sorbet au Fruit de Kiwi

### Filet de Boeuf en Croûte
Sauce Périgourdine
*Clos-Vougeot Domaine des Varoïlles 1975*

### Salade de Saison

### Fromage
*Warre's Port 1966*

### Charlotte Suisse

### Pouding de Noël à l'Anglaise

### Café et Friandises
*Cognac Grande Fine Champagne*
*Liqueur Elizir Pear Williams*

Maitre de Salle
Jacques Amblard

Maitre Queux
Hubert Winkler

tation in the field of culinary arts will be laid bare before the guest.

After the chef selects the menu, the diner must understand that each item will have its own individual character and taste. An interrelationship is necessary for the right impact on the taste buds, together with concerns of sweet, sour, bitter or salty qualities, and aesthetics. Cocktails and smoking should be avoided prior to the dinner; these reduce the sensitivity of the taste buds. All selections, served in small amounts, must relate to each other for a memorable evening of rare experience.

After careful planning, Purchasing is invited to discuss the availability of particular items (sometimes many weeks in advance), quantity, quality, and estimated cost. At this point, Purchasing becomes a part of the planning team. Next, the wine steward is invited to discuss the wine selection vital to any gourmet dinner; again, availability, quantity, quality, and cost. The support chefs now join in the planning and assume their areas of responsibility. All details are examined at this time. Staff operations follow, such as Commissary, Receiving, and Storage.

With these communications in place and responsibilities established, the Dining Rooms management joins the group. These persons will serve the dinner. Silver needs, twenty or so pieces for each guest, will be covered; the person in charge of the silver will become invaluable at this point. Agreement will be reached on china, the number and types of wine glasses, availability of linens, number of napkins, table items such as flowers, and menus in both French and English. The number of guests will be discussed and table assignments made. Communication and training for waitresses and captains are arranged. Timing is essential for each course in preparation and serving.

Two fears arise. The chef is concerned that the service group will not properly execute the dinner. The headwaiter is concerned that the kitchen operations will break down. These fears are known as the back and front concerns; they have always been present and always will be.

Let us suppose it is now four days before the big evening. The executive chef is in daily contact with Purchasing. Will all items arrive? Are there alternate suppliers? As the food begins to come, the chef will inspect each item for freshness, quality, and size. He will call the wine steward about the wine courses. The tempo begins to increase. Tests are being made and rehearsals begin.

It is now the day! No one goes near the chef. Pressures are tremendous. Many cooks and trainees have arrived to observe the preparations. No one speaks. The concentration of the chef amazes the cooks. By 7:30 p.m. the guests have arrived. As they are seated, the ladies in beautiful gowns escorted by their gentlemen in formal dress, we are reminded of the gala opening of the Green Room in January 1913. The tables are ablaze with silver. The memorable experience begins.

It is now 11:30 p.m., and the affair is winding down. Gaiety, happiness, and fellowship are present throughout the room. No one can believe four hours have passed by so quickly. The final course is served. In the kitchens the executive chef sits down, totally drained both physically and emotionally. He will not appear in the dining room to be introduced, since he feels that all his employees should be so honored, and many have gone home. He removes his tall white hat, thanks everyone, and slowly leaves his domain. "Good night, Chef!" The evening has shown the art of cooking at its finest.

# Buffets

A buffet is sometimes referred to as a smorgasbord, hunt breakfast, or groaning board. The Hotel du Pont, for over forty years, has enjoyed an outstanding reputation for its buffets. This reputation is very important, because in recent years the number of buffets in the Wilmington area has grown steadily. Restaurants have different reasons for offering such service, and menus range from the most lavish gourmet presentation to a modest salad table.

Why and when did elaborate buffets become a part of food service in the Hotel du Pont? The Thursday Night Buffet served in the Green Room was the first. Years ago in many households, Thursday was the traditional day off for the maid or cook, and this is still true today to a lesser degree. So on Thursday evenings Father would invite the family out for dinner. Many guests did not want the formality of ordering from menus, and the children wanted to see and select the food themselves. With plenty for all at one price it was, and is, a family affair.

The Sunday Brunch Buffet was introduced in 1964 after studies were made to find alternatives to improve the guest count in the Green Room on Sundays. These reports covered the guest mix, ages, number of couples, ladies, families, and children, the amount of the average check, and more. The absence of families was disturbing. A Sunday Brunch was developed to be more than a breakfast attraction: it would offer the main meal of the day, a buffet for the family after church. From the beginning, the community's response was immediate. Today, this affair attracts guests from great distances. Nearly six hundred guests come each Sunday, and many more cannot be accommodated. Sunday Brunch at the Hotel has become almost a family tradition.

Seven years ago, the Wednesday Buffet was initiated through an accident. On one particular day the Green Room was completely booked for lunch. At 10:30 a.m., a pipe broke in the floor of the basement which caused gas to leak into the Green Room's air conditioning system. To use this room for lunch would be impossible. A decision was made quickly to set up a modest buffet in the du Barry Room. At lunchtime the headwaiter of the Green Room greeted the guests, explained the emergency, and directed them to the du Barry Room. Most of the guests were quite agreeable to the buffet. In fact, they liked it so much that many asked, why not a buffet every week in the Green Room? Wednesday thus became the day for the buffet lunch. This affair has become very popular and has increased the guest count on Wednesdays by forty percent, all because of a broken pipe.

Every buffet begins with a planning session. The buffet chef, sometimes called the garde manger, is in charge, with representatives from Purchasing and the Commissary, the pastry chef, the Dining Rooms manager, and support personnel attending. What will be the theme (buffets provide great flexibility), the degree of showmanship? What about the location of food (always the "highest quality"), quantity, cost, areas of responsibility, number of hot and cold items, cookery at the table, color, attractiveness, eye appeal, pastry table, number of cream-filled items, ice sculpture, dress code, relief personnel? Meetings are held with all preparation and serving employees to discuss items by name and the production forecast. The buffet must be elegant but simple at the same time.

Portions of all items served on a buffet are frozen for one week afterwards in compliance with food sanitation procedures. All foods, with few exceptions, are discarded after the meal period. Unfortunately, some people believe that buffets are used to merchandise leftovers. No respectable restaurant would entertain such a policy.

Buffets are prepared for self-service. Let us suggest that the guest first visit the table without selecting any items, so that he may be sure of the menu. Then he should take small quantities and not overload his plate, since he may return as often as he wishes. Of those who overeat, who consume three or four large platters of food, such as twenty eggs at the Sunday Brunch, or a dozen pastries, the Hotel is only concerned for their health and good judgment.

A buffet is a classic, a great challenge to a chef and his associates. There, at that table, his artistic talents are set forth. His total culinary ability is spread before the appreciative guest.

# The Bake Shop

In the great bake shops around the world, a little sign sometimes appears in the windows:

In your mouth for ten seconds,
In your stomach for five hours,
On your hips for the rest of your life!

Historically, bake shops in hotels, while independent, have been a part of the kitchen operation. While pastry and food preparation chefs have respect for one another, they think and live in different worlds. Associations are friendly, but formal.

From the beginning, the highest professional standards were established for years to come at the Hotel and are evident today. A retired baker with over forty years of service was asked what had impressed him most during his long tenure (he had missed only one day's work). After a long pause, he said, "Always the highest quality, no short cuts." As it was then, it is today.

The executive pastry chef is supported by a pastry chef and twelve highly trained bakers. While the city sleeps, the bakers are busy around the clock preparing the many delights for the next day. All bakery products are produced daily; no additives are used. The Hotel's bakery is one of the few in the country to use heavy cream in its production.

Many guests still remember the famous and rich ice cream made by the bake shop, which they enjoyed so much. It was removed from the menu because it was overportioned and underpriced. This ice cream is again in production; however, its portions and price have been corrected.

All too often, the artistic ability of the chefs is not understood or appreciated. The creativity, knowledge, and skills for a chef to produce a wedding cake that reflects the wishes of the bride and the cultural background surrounding the ceremony are very complex. During the current executive chef's career, he worked in a prestigious hotel in Hong Kong. His most memorable experience occurred when a prominent family rented the entire hotel for a wedding reception, to which six thousand guests were invited. To set the tone for the party, the pastry shop developed an enormous wedding cake, to be placed in front of the hotel, through which the guests would drive on arrival. The support frame was made by the carpentry shop and covered with sugar decorated in the appropriate colors. When asked what all that cost, the chef answered, "The family was very rich."

As just one example of the chef's artistic ability, the Hotel du Pont once hosted a Chinese wedding. The wedding cake, a pagoda, told a story of happiness. The cake was six layers high, seven feet tall, and each floor part of a separate story. It weighed eighty pounds, plus another forty pounds of special sugar. Decorations were selected carefully: red for happiness, gold for good fortune, green for abundance in life. White could not be used; it is the Oriental color for mourning. To think that the result of four or five days of planning and preparation, so meaningful to the bride and groom and their families, was consumed by the guests in a short time, only to be remembered from a photograph.

# Beverages

During 1912, the discussion covering facilities required for the sale of alcoholic beverages included a wholesale wine and liquor department. The wine cellar would be located next to the ice-making equipment in the basement under the Men's Café and Bar along Market Street. Some thought the cellar, at times, might need increased cooling. In 1913, this wine cellar was stocked with the finest wines from Europe, and Percy Harbison came from England to take charge of the operation. Under his leadership, the Hotel acquired one of the finest wine cellars in the country.

Mr. Harbison guarded the wine cellar as though it contained precious jewels, which indeed it did. The best wines were imported from all over Europe; huge casks of liquor were received, decorked, and bottled under his supervision. A bottle of this beverage labeled "Hotel Special Rye Whiskey" was loaned to the Hotel for exhibit in its modest museum. The bottle was sealed, so no evaluation has been made of its contents.

In the latter part of 1919, many organizations supporting the enactment of the Eighteenth Amendment to the Constitution met in the Gold Ballroom. Speakers for these affairs were ladies of the W.C.T.U., elected officials, and businessmen. Standing ovations were given these speakers as they set forth all the evils of alcohol. Not known by those attending was the fact that many of the speakers proceeded to a room set up to enjoy these evils and, in some cases, others were more bold and went directly to the Men's Café and Bar.

In January 1920, the Prohibition Act was approved, and it made the sale of alcoholic beverages illegal. This law meant many changes in the Hotel's operations. The Men's Café and Bar closed. The Grille, the elegant gathering place in Wilmington for dancing and dining nightly, opened for lunch only. The priceless collection of beverages found its way into many private cellars in the Wilmington area when, on the night the act went into effect, automobiles were lined up along 11th Street and were filled with case after case of liquor and wine. Many of the bellmen complained they were too young to handle the goods. By the next morning, the wine cellar was empty. After the inventory was disposed of, Mr. Harbison purchased a farm near Kennett Square, Pennsylvania, and retired. Some say he continued his interest in wines and liquors, strictly as a consultant.

A well-known Wilmington bootlegger delivered whiskey to the Hotel in dress boxes and men's clothing boxes marked with the emblems of prominent Wilmington stores. This ploy worked well for some time until an alert bellman decided that a lot of clothing was being purchased by Hotel guests.

Three-Gun Wilson, a federal agent assigned to the Hotel to observe any violation of the Prohibition Act, slept most of the time. A group of bootleggers rented six rooms on the second floor to set up their illegal operation. The whiskey was received by boat downriver near Delaware City. Within four days, federal agents raided the rooms and ended this operation.

Pierre S. du Pont was very conservative concerning the use of alcohol. He liked to drink in moderation and thought that his and others' rights were being violated by the total ban. He did not believe the Prohibition Act had been effective and, in fact, he worked vigorously for its repeal. With the repeal of the act in 1933, Mr. du Pont provided leadership in developing laws for administering the sale of alcoholic beverages. He was impressed with Swiss laws and their application, and many of the liquor laws on the books of Delaware today were instigated by Mr. du Pont and closely related to those followed by the Swiss. He became chairman of the Delaware State Alcoholic Beverage Commission.

On one occasion, Mr. du Pont arrived in the Green Room for lunch precisely at 11:45 a.m. Seeing a fancy portable bar, he asked its purpose. He was told that it would be used to improve service and promote beverage sales. Mr. du Pont commented, "I am not sure we want to promote alcoholic beverage sales at lunch. This room is used primarily by businessmen and, in fact, that arrangement looks unsafe." The bar was removed by 2:00 p.m.

Over the years, the Hotel du Pont has been looked upon as the social hub of Wilmington. Its location may suggest it as a meeting place for drinks, but this is not so. For a hotel of three hundred rooms, it is conservative or even moderate in the sale of alcohol. Historically, sales in this area average ten percent of the Hotel's total sales. The Hotel opened a retail liquor store in December 1933 and closed it in March 1940; from all accounts, the Hotel was never identified as a place to purchase retail beverages. The business community represents a large segment of the total sales, particularly during the week, and three-martini and lavish lunches for businessmen rarely occur in the Hotel. It would be reasonable to conclude that any person following this practice would not be an executive for very long.

During the last ten or fifteen years, drinking habits have changed drastically, particularly in wine sales. Ten years ago, the sale of sixty bottles of wine per week by the Hotel was considered good. Today, approximately 1,600 bottles are sold. White wines are favored by nearly eighty percent of the guests. The increase in sales of wine has resulted in a substantial decrease in sales of other beverages.

# THE WHOLESALE WINE AND LIQUOR DEPARTMENT
## HOTEL DU PONT, WILMINGTON, DEL.

## SPECIAL COMBINATION CASES AT ATTRACTIVE PRICES

### Each Article is the Best of its Kind at the Price

**Combination No. 1—Special Price $3.50.**

| | |
|---|---|
| 1 Bottle Top Notch Whiskey | 1.00 |
| 1 Bottle Caton Club Whiskey | .75 |
| 1 Bottle California Sherry | .50 |
| 1 Bottle California Port | .50 |
| 1 Bottle Pilot Dry Gin | .75 |
| 1 Bottle Italian Vermouth (Imported) | .75 |
| 6 | 4.25 |

**Combination No. 2—Special Price $5.00.**

| | |
|---|---|
| 1 Bottle Hotel Special Whiskey | 1.50 |
| 1 Bottle Top Notch Whiskey | 1.00 |
| 1 Bottle Vino de Pasto Sherry (Imported) | 1.00 |
| 1 Bottle Oliva Port (Imported) | 1.00 |
| 1 Bottle Hotel Superior Gin | 1.00 |
| 1 Bottle Italian Vermouth (Imported) | .75 |
| 6 | 6.25 |

**Combination No. 3—Special Price $6.50.**

| | |
|---|---|
| 2 Bottles Hotel Special Whiskey | 3.00 |
| 1 Bottle Cognac Brandy (Imported) | 1.75 |
| 1 Bottle Old London Dock Jamaica Rum (Imported) | 1.25 |
| 2 Bottles Claret, Medoc (Domestic) | 1.00 |
| 2 Bottles Romano Sherry (Domestic) | 1.50 |
| 2 Bottles Fine Old Port (Domestic) | 1.50 |
| 2 Bottles Rhine Wine | 1.00 |
| 12 | 11.00 |

**Combination No. 4—Special Price $10.50.**

| | |
|---|---|
| 1 Bottle Bordeaux (White), Graves (Imported) | 1.00 |
| 1 Bottle Bordeaux (Red), Floriac (Imported) | 1.00 |
| 1 Bottle Port Olivia (Imported) | 1.00 |
| 1 Bottle Vino de Pasto Sherry (Imported) | 1.00 |
| 1 Bottle Top Notch Whiskey | 1.00 |
| 1 Bottle Hotel Superior Dry Gin | 1.00 |
| 1 Bottle Blackberry (Best) | 1.00 |
| 1 Bottle London Dock Jamaica Rum (Imported) | 1.25 |
| 1 Bottle Martini Cocktails | 1.00 |
| 1 Bottle Manhattan Cocktails | 1.00 |
| 1 Bottle Hotel Superior Scotch | 1.35 |
| 1 Bottle Brotherhood Champagne, E. D. | 1.25 |
| 12 | 12.85 |

### THE CARE OF WINE.

The process of uncorking Champagne is frequently mismanaged. The cork should be slowly and noiselessly extracted after, first the wire, and then the string, are entirely removed. The glass must be near at hand so that no wine may be lost. Care should be taken that the wine flows slowly. If gently poured on the side of the glass the flow will be checked and the glass filled without spilling. Do not fill the glass to the brim, but leave a quarter of an inch or more free. Rich Champagne only requires to be stood in ice to the shoulder of the bottle, not longer than twenty minutes, even in the hottest weather. It is important to remember that too much icing destroys body and vinosity.

We cannot too strongly impress upon our customers, in handling Champagne, the importance of keeping the bottles on their side until required for use. A disregard of this will render flat the most effervescent wines.

Burgundy, Claret, Sherry and Port require special attention. Their temperature should be about 60 degrees and, when poured into glasses, the bottle should be steadily handled, so that any sediment that may be in the bottom of the bottle is not disturbed. Bottles containing these wines, when laid away, should be placed on their sides to keep the corks moist.

### Average Strength of Various Wines, Etc.

| | Alcohol | | Alcohol |
|---|---|---|---|
| Burgundy | 13% | Bordeaux | 11% |
| Champagne | 12% | Rhine | 11% |
| Sherry | 19% | Hungarian | 13% |
| Port | 22% | Burton Ale | 8% |
| Madeira | 18% | Porter | 6% |
| Marsala | 24% | California Claret | 12% |

### WHAT TO DRINK AND WHY.

Take SHERRY with your meals—you will find it an excellent stimulant and an aid to digestion.

CLARET will make a torpid liver live anew and urge it on to properly perform its important functions.

People who are inclined to stoutness need not go through the laborious task of dieting if they will but drink WHITE WINES with their meals. They positively assist in reducing flesh.

PORT WINE will turn into rich, life-giving blood that will make you strong and vigorous.

TOKAY WINE is really a wonderful aid to the mother who is nursing. It gives her system the nourishment it needs. Convalescents who drink Tokay Wine will quickly regain their lost strength.

WHISKEY will revive one who is faint and needs a stimulant. It should be considered indispensable to the medicine chest of a well-regulated household.

BRANDY is the doctor's ever-ready prescription for patients too sick to retain any other form of nourishment.

GIN rouses sluggish kidneys and makes them fulfill the duties intended by nature.

RUM will break up a cold more quickly than any favorite prescription of a druggist. It should be served as a hot punch.

CHAMPAGNE is excellent for the stomach.

SCOTCH WHISKEY is noted for its benevolent action upon the lungs.

BLACKBERRY BRANDY is a well-known household remedy for dysentery.

This early beverage price list has medical advice for the reader . . . and competitive prices!

A few comments on our history and consumption of beverages may be meaningful. Early drinking habits by the founders of our country were not considered at all sophisticated. Benjamin Franklin said, "Wine is a constant proof that God loves us and loves to see us happy." Wine was made before history began to be recorded; it has given comfort, pleasure, and exhilaration to humanity for thousands of years and will continue to do so. Imported wines in the early days were expensive. Therefore, beer, whiskey, and rum became the primary drinks. Breweries opened in America as early as 1637; rye and barley whiskeys were produced by small distilleries located up and down the Atlantic coast; rum was imported in large quantities from the Caribbean islands. The Whiskey Rebellion did not deter those who distilled a beverage which became well known, lawfully and unlawfully, as "corn likker."

Wine production in our country was encouraged over two hundred years ago in California by Father Junipero Serra, a Franciscan friar of great vision. As the Spanish moved north from Mexico, they established a chain of missions and planted vines of Spanish grapes called "mission grapes." These grapes produced sacramental wines for the churches and table wines for the friars and travellers who moved north along the Mission Trail.

Why the trend to wines? Thousands of our soldiers stationed in Europe during World War II spent many months in the wine-growing countries, and the increase in travel by American tourists to these countries has raised our exposure to nations consuming great quantities of wine. Our own country has made great progress since Prohibition in the development of vineyards and wine making. American wines are now competing successfully with European wines. Training programs for waiters and captains now teach them how to suggest and serve wine properly. Wine adds to dining pleasure, is low in alcoholic content, costs less than liquor, and creates a ceremonial atmosphere.

The increased demands for a greater variety of wines may make it necessary for the Hotel again to establish a wine cellar. Should this take place, it may be appropriate to name it "The Percy Harbison Wine Cellar."

# The Banquet Department

Before discussing the Banquet area, it would be well to review the background of two men who made great contributions to the organization and growth of the Banquet Department from 1927 to 1969: William J. Mitchell and M. P. C. Nielsen.

During the formative years of the Hotel, food service in the public and private rooms was identified as the Restaurant Department. One of the early managers was William J. Mitchell, known to the public and employees as Mitch. Later, his title would be changed to maitre d'hôtel. The leadership he provided would soon make the Hotel du Pont a byword of those patrons who expected high quality, excellent service, and pleasure in dining.

Before Mitch joined the Hotel in 1927, he received a wealth of training and experience in many of the outstanding hotels and country clubs in the country. His training began in New York as a bus boy with Delmonico's, then as waiter and headwaiter at the Hotel Taft and the Duchess House. Advancement, new experiences, and responsibilities came in such clubs as The Westchester, Laurel-in-the-Pines, and Glen Ridge. "All of this moving around would seem to indicate I was unable to keep a job. It was the method in those days. You changed position to gain specific training. Many professionals still follow this practice today. Individually, I learned a great deal from each location. Collectively, it qualified me to become the maitre d'hôtel of the Hotel du Pont." Mitch's personal concern for training others would have a profound effect on the growth of the Banquet area and the professionalism of the employees. It was his practice after each large party to gather his staff to review the evening's performance. Further investigation indicates it was also to enjoy a moment of fellowship helped out by a few rounds of libations.

On Mitch's retirement in 1947, his assistant, M. P. C. Nielsen, was named maitre d'hôtel of the Hotel du Pont. Max had been born in Denmark. While serving in the army, he attended school and learned accounting and later worked in a cooperative general store. Times were very bad and jobs were few in Denmark. Max had read about opportunities in America. Since he had a sister living in New York, he decided to seek his fortune in a new country and landed in New York in September 1926, with very little money. He discovered that jobs were available in hotels in Atlantic City, New Jersey, and hired on, knowing that at least he would be able to eat in that profession. His apprenticeship began as a bus boy trainee in the Hotel Ambassador, where he was later promoted to chief bus boy in charge of forty bus boys, an increase in responsibilities with no increase in pay. Subsequently he was employed by the Ritz-Carlton and the Shelburne Hotels as a waiter in training. During this apprenticeship, Max learned all types of silver service, room arrangements, plating of foods, food quality, guest and employee relations, knowledge of food costs, and the importance of communicating guests' comments to the food preparation chefs.

In May 1930, he joined the Hotel du Pont as a waiter in the Green Room. Promotions followed, to scrub captain and then captain. As maitre d'hôtel, Max became known as an outstanding professional. He was a very formal person, always impeccably dressed, clicking his heels and bowing graciously whenever he greeted someone. He quickly put guests at ease, making them feel comfortable and welcome. The Danish accent was always present.

Max followed a routine of his own while planning a social function, say, a wedding reception. Nothing would be on Max's desk except the function order and a pencil held in the palms of his hands. "Please review with me your plans. I want you to know that the Hotel is honored that you want this meaningful affair in the Hotel du Pont." As the young couple outlined the reception, Max would say, "Why, that's delightful, just beautiful," always rolling that pencil between his palms. When the couple finished, Max then asked, "How much money do you plan to spend per invited guest?" With some hesitation, the amount was stated. The pencil dropped to the function order for the moment of concern, the total cost. "Why, that's 50¢ more than you planned; however, I've been so impressed with your plans that I'll reduce the cost by 25¢." The couple were excited and pleased that the Hotel would reduce the cost just for them.

One of the questions most asked of Max by visitors was, "What are your most memorable experiences over the years in planning the wide range of social and civic affairs?" Max replied, "I hesitate to answer such a question. Such affairs are private and that trust must be honored. I will comment in a general way on but two. One involved the eightieth birthday celebration for Irénée du Pont in the Gold Ballroom in December 1956. Members of his family, including his eight children, made all the arrangements and took an active part in the planning. Many of his thirty-five grandchildren also had duties to perform. Three hundred members of the du Pont family were invited, a rare occasion to have so many members of the family present. To be a part of that evening, to see Mr. du Pont, who seemed to love everyone and enjoy every moment and who was indeed the star of his own party, was rare for me and a night I will never forget."

When asked what experiences he encountered in planning so many social and civic affairs with the Du Pont family, Max commented, "I have been privileged to work with the family on both very complex and relatively simple affairs. Some have been large and others quite small. It would be rare for any activity they plan not to have a theme of simplicity and comfort. The family is always well prepared with all details in place; the final part of the affair is the cost. It would be difficult for me to remember when Du Pont family members failed to be knowledgeable and efficient."

The other memorable affair was the celebration in the Gold Ballroom of the dedication of the Delaware-New Jersey Memorial Bridge in 1951. Two hundred fifty guests were to be invited to a buffet dinner with prime ribs of beef as the entrée. During the ten days prior to the dedication, the list grew to eight hundred guests. "I will not go into all the details. You have often heard of the planning and professionalism of the Hotel staff. It was my finest moment in both of these areas with the help of the arranging committee. It was a total success." Over those twenty-one years the Banquet area would enjoy great growth, professionalism, and an excellent reputation because young Max had decided to leave his home in Denmark and come to America.

The Banquet operation, until recently known as the Catering Department, administers one of the largest and most complex divisions in the Hotel. Nearly 5,000 privately arranged affairs take place each year for 150,000 guests. Fourteen banquet rooms accommodate these large numbers. The functions range in guest size from very few to as many as 700. The staff to arrange and serve these guests requires seventy employees, excluding food preparation personnel. Half of the affairs, primarily business luncheons, are arranged by telephone. A third have had confirmed reservations covering a period of twenty-five years. Many organizations have maintained reservations for forty years and twenty groups for over sixty years.

Why not ask Bernd Mayer, the present Banquet manager, "What are your primary responsibilities?" Each morning on his desk are three sets of function orders. First, he will evaluate all phases of performance involving the previous day's activity; second, review and discuss this day's functions with the chef and his staff; third, review and discuss last minute changes affecting the next day's affairs. These are known in a manager's life as the past, present, and future.

Three important basics must be understood by all personnel working on a function: a precise language spoken and heard by all involved in the execution of the affair; the critical importance of timing; and once the affair begins, only two persons involved in its conduct, the host or hostess and the headwaiter.

"Follow up, assume nothing, check again and again." Arrangements for each affair require detailed planning and follow-up. A function order must be prepared for each activity. This function order, plus a daily news communication, will be distributed to the twenty service operations that may be involved in the execution of the affair. Arrangements for a large lavish party will require six meetings with the host (average time two hours), dozens of telephone calls, at least ten meetings with the food preparation personnel, service support, and the wine steward. During these discussions, which are long and complex, two highly important relationships develop: the host comes to know the Banquet manager professionally and gains confidence in his ability and knowledge; and the Banquet manager comes to understand the host's personality and wishes so he can more easily evaluate the host's priorities, likes, and dislikes. In other words, a fine relationship is established which makes possible a memorable occasion.

A dinner for four to five hundred guests requires forty employees to serve it. While each one is an individual, all must perform collectively as one, with only twenty minutes to serve and twenty minutes to clear the tables. One guest was heard to say, "Choreographically, you think the execution of the service is so quiet, professional, and well-coordinated, it equals that of a great ballet. Everybody comes to expect that at the Hotel."

The Banquet managers have found that the ladies of our city over the years have given many hours of their time to charitable causes. The primary objective of the incoming chairman of an organization is to make more money than the previous chairman. During the negotiations with the Hotel, the preparations and the agenda for discussion are well rehearsed. These ladies seem to feel that any charges made for service by the Hotel will impair the well-being of the community. One chairman, when asked how much money she hoped to have left over out of each dollar of sales, replied without the slightest hesitation, "all of it!"

During one of these negotiations, the chairman requested more space; in particular, the du Barry Room. "We know this room is booked for the period we need, but do you mind if we discuss the matter with those who have engaged the room?" The Hotel objected to any such action. The chairman replied, "Well, do you object if we try pillow talk?" To the Hotel's knowledge, this question has not been answered to date. The Hotel has made no investigation into the matter. Incidentally, the room was not made available. The community is richer because of these ladies, and indeed the Hotel is.

Where will all the functions take place?

### GOLD BALLROOM

Over the years, this prestigious room has been reserved by individuals and organizations from all levels of society. It has been transformed into castles, residences, and gardens for elegant social affairs that astound the imagination. The most prominent in fashionable society have entertained here at the

Bachelors' Ball, debutante parties, bar mitzvahs, weddings; governmental gatherings have honored presidents and members of royal families; hospital boards, the Junior League, churches, and many other charitable organizations have held antiques shows, balls, follies, and other affairs to raise money for community needs. A Wilmington based television station held a fund-raising gala, as have politicians and others too numerous to name. Organizers of events find the Hotel's personality so pronounced that it absorbs all types of people, which means that the most heterogeneous elements feel happy under its roof.

Many ask, why is the Ballroom located so far from the kitchen? Early plans for its use did not include food service. For the first social affair, Lester Lanin, a society orchestra, furnished the music. It would appear many times in future years. One of the next large social affairs involved the Guy Lombardo and Vincent Lopez orchestras. There was continuous music for dancing, and 25,000 freshly cut flowers were delivered for decorations. Bellmen were used for checking and were told to dress in tuxedos and wear white gloves. Why white gloves? To protect the ladies' furs. One bellman reported that some of those furs had not received very good attention, since he had to change his gloves four times during the evening. Many great social affairs would follow, with most of the big name bands and magnificent decorations.

Some of the decorations were so elaborate that they threatened the beautiful craftsmanship and painting on the walls of the Ballroom. On November 11, 1925, R. R. M. Carpenter, chairman of the Hotel Du Pont Co., wrote a letter to the Executive Committee of the Du Pont Company to point out this danger. A resolution instructed Hotel management to forbid any decorations or flowers from touching the walls or ceiling of the room. Many people wanting to rent the Ballroom objected to these restrictions. However, Mr. Carpenter's rule is still in effect today.

J. Liddon Pennock, a florist from Philadelphia, is one of the most noted floral designers on the East Coast. Over the years, Mr. Pennock on many occasions has been responsible for the decoration of the Gold Ballroom for the most lavish affairs. When asked to comment on the Ballroom, he answered, "This room is so beautiful one has little to do."

The Kiwanis Club of Wilmington was the first organization to reserve the Ballroom, in 1919. The speaker was Governor Charles Goldsborough of Maryland and the subject, *Value of Cooperation*. The first convention held was a regional meeting for undertakers. The room was filled with caskets. The bellmen, who disliked the night manager, decided to dress a bellman in a shroud and place him in a casket. Later that night, the manager was notified of a noise in the Gold Ballroom. During the investigation, sounds were heard coming from a casket. As the manager approached, the bellman rose up. The manager fainted, and for a short time it was thought he would need a casket on a permanent basis. Employee relations improved after that.

The room has been leased for affairs not usually associated with ballrooms. The Philadelphia Phillies major league baseball club exercised there during World War II. A dog show also took place. The function report indicated that the manners of the dogs were superior; nevertheless, the records do not show the room used again for this purpose. Automobile shows were booked several times, and a window had to be removed to accommodate the cars.

During Christmas week the Masonic Club of Wilmington holds its annual Christmas luncheon. One year a number of senior citizens attended, as well as forty children selected from families unable to afford to celebrate Christmas. The Ballroom was decorated gaily, and in the front of the room was a platform with a big chair for Santa Claus, surrounded by lots of presents. Just before lunchtime, the children arrived, accompanied by a Salvation Army leader. They held hands, tense and uncomfortable, eyes big and round, not a smile; none of them had ever been in the Hotel du Pont before. As they entered the foyer of the Ballroom, club members dressed like elves and clowns greeted them and escorted them to their tables near the platform. The children now began to relax. After a festive lunch, bells were heard in the distance and into the room came Santa and his helpers. Taking his seat, he called each child's name to come forward. He talked to everyone and gave them clothing and other gifts, possibly the only gifts they would receive over the Christmas holidays. As the children left, laughing and clutching their presents, should you ever have asked or had a doubt about Santa Claus, at that moment you would have been sure. It was a great moment for the children, the Masonic Club, our community, and the Hotel du Pont. Merry Christmas to all!

During the latter part of May each year, many of the high schools hold their senior proms in the Ballroom. These dances attract nearly 7,000 young men and women. The young ladies are beautifully dressed in colorful gowns, corsages in place, lovely as they radiate a special dimension of happiness. Each one seems to realize this milestone in her life. Their escorts, without knowing, are looking at their sweethearts with endearment and admiration. They are dressed formally and carefully, not even one pair of shoes needs polishing. Many will have dinner in the dining rooms, sometimes ordered and arranged for by their parents. With few exceptions, the whole celebration is happy and unforgettable in an atmosphere of great dignity. Some of these young people later will want to have their wedding receptions in this sentimental and memory filled room. Three generations in one family now have held their wedding receptions in the Gold Ballroom.

### DU BARRY ROOM

This room is used today by the Banquet operation for large affairs in conjunction with the Ballroom. However, because of its beauty, location, superb planning, and architecture, it enjoys on its own the distinction of being the most reserved room in the Hotel. It is comfortable for a dinner party of fifteen or one hundred fifty, and it is perfect for small dances and cocktail parties.

On occasion the Executive Committee of the Du Pont Company has lunch and invites other members of management as guests. For each affair a small menu card is placed on each table. At one such lunch the menu card, although proofread by three different persons, read, "Long Island Dickling." Afterward, one telephone caller remarked, "We are pleased that the food served exceeds your ability to spell." A note received said, "Should you be unable to spell 'duck,' you are in a bad way." When the typist was asked how she could possibly make such an error, especially for the Executive Committee's luncheon, she replied, "What is the Executive Committee?"

The Hotel over the years has taken great pride in its professionalism and execution of privately arranged affairs. A dinner party was planned by a group representing a university. The purpose was to entertain a person of great importance to the institution. It was to be a very formal affair, an eight course gourmet dinner, with flowers for the ladies and flowers at each table for six, string music, waitresses in white gloves, and a headwaiter and captain present throughout. At the conclusion of the dinner, the light level was raised and the guest of honor introduced. As he stood to speak, a rock band, in the Gold Ballroom below the du Barry Room, went into action using eight six-foot high amplifiers to provide dance music for 450 young men and women. The volume shook the corner of 11th and Orange Streets; the chandelier in the du Barry Room began to sway. The hostess rushed down to the Ballroom to ask for cooperation, without success. Needless to say, on the next morning the committee who arranged the affair met with the staff of the Hotel. There were no interruptions as each member of the committee disassembled the place. No minutes or recordings were made, but you can be sure that the discussion of the disaster would linger in the minds of the staff for years to come.

## PRIVATE DINING ROOMS

Seven private dining rooms were available in 1913. These rooms, known as parlors and identified by letters of the alphabet, were located on the Mezzanine floor. Most of the rooms were small, although one could accommodate fifty guests. They were finished in Circassian walnut and furnished with custom-made furniture. The space since has been taken over for other purposes.

During 1937, a private dining suite was established on the eleventh floor facing east and overlooking the three rivers so important in the history of Wilmington. Georgian in style and decoration, it was named the Georgian Suite and would be known as the Executive Dining Room, to be used only by corporate executives of the Du Pont Company. Over the years, this need diminished, and it was made available to serve the growing needs of the Banquet operation. Thirty-nine years later, it would be renovated. The alterations included the installation of a preparation pantry, enlarged lounge facilities, a service bar, a change in the color scheme to that of our state (yellow and blue), and a new name: the Delaware Suite. Like so many facilities in the Hotel, it has its own character. For many Delawareans, it is their very special place in the sky. At night, as guests look at the stars and the lights of Wilmington and the New Jersey shoreline, they enjoy an endless view wrapped in a celestial sphere, heavenly indeed.

As the guest enters the second floor private dining area and sees the crystal chandeliers glistening over the red carpeted corridors, he experiences a feeling of expectation. Handsome antiques and original paintings add warmth to the beautifully furnished rooms, which differ in size and style. Several are decorated in shades of red, white, and blue. Two have been designed for the use of the department heads and of the Executive Committee of the Du Pont Company, but they may be leased for parties when not needed for their primary function.

It is fair to say no hotel in America has private dining rooms comparable to these in furnishings, attractiveness, and privacy. They provide an atmosphere of aesthetic pleasure, the essence of taste for social or business use.

A headwaiter was in charge of a festive birthday celebration attended by longstanding patrons of the Hotel. The host asked the headwaiter, "When is the Hotel going to pick up the check?" The headwaiter, with a smile, assured him "today." With that, the host and guests all thanked him and departed. This check represented a substantial amount of money. The headwaiter found his way to the manager's office to report the matter. The manager simply decided, "You can afford to pay this check, and I know all of the guests will be most grateful." No repetition of such an offer has occurred since.

The Banquet area once received a call to reserve a dining room for lunch for twenty-five guests. A gourmet menu was ordered, with magnums of champagne: Frank Sinatra was coming to town. In her excitement, the Hotel's sales representative failed to follow long-established procedures when such reservations are made. She called friends in the nearby office buildings, and in turn they called friends. The press found out, and at noon the Lobby was filled with people hoping to see the great Sinatra. Everything was in order, the menu ready, the champagne chilling, the waitresses ready. It was 12:15 p.m., then 12:30 p.m., and still no call from the arranger. At 12:45 p.m., all faces of the Hotel management were red. The Hotel had been hoaxed: Mr. Sinatra was not in Wilmington. The press enjoyed it. The sales representative's greatest concern was that she did not get to see her idol. Someone reported she now is employed by a boutique.

One headwaiter, with over thirty years' service, said his greatest moment was to serve six Du Pont Company presidents at once at a private luncheon in these rooms. In attendance were Walter S. Carpenter, Crawford H. Greenewalt, Lammot du Pont Copeland, Charles B. McCoy, Edward R. Kane, and

Irving S. Shapiro. This indeed was a rare and unforgettable experience.

The president of a large French company and his associates were entertained for dinner in a private dining room. After the meal, the president through an interpreter thanked the host and said, "It is not often that one gets a meal in the United States that convinces a Frenchman that you can get good meals here. This was magnificent!"

*The Lobby*

Photo by George G. Cambanes
for the Du Pont Photo Studio

*A view of the Kitchen*

*Executive Pastry Chef Josef A. Burch
poses with a spectacular Chinese Wedding cake*

Photo by Frederick P. Ristine III
for the Du Pont Photo Studio

*Hubert M. Winkler, Executive Chef, presiding at the buffet table*

*The Sussex Room*

*A typical bedroom*

*The entrance to the Gold Ballroom suite is executed in travertine and roseal marble. The ceiling is gold leaf and the balustrade is bronze and polished steel.*

*e Playhouse*

*Atop the pillars in the Grille gnomes watch over the room, ensuring each guest's safety*

Behind the Scene

# The Housekeeping Department

During the opening of the Hotel in 1913, the first executive housekeeper was Margaret T. MacManus, a native of Ireland. She was a quiet-spoken, demure little woman. Professionally trained, she came to the Hotel du Pont from the Hotel Taft in New York. Any question on hotel housekeeping in this country or Europe could be answered from her wealth of knowledge. During her early training, she served as a lady's maid to a German baroness. She described her career as "making people comfortable."

Here at the Hotel du Pont she was considered very exacting and strict by the maids. All maids living in the Hotel were at least twenty-one years old, but it was necessary for them to obtain a pass to leave at night. They had to return no later than 11 p.m. for bed check. Should anyone miss bed check, she was summoned to the linen room, known as the execution room, to explain why to Miss MacManus.

She soon became known as "Mom Mom." One of her favorite activities was to act as a matchmaker for this group of lovely maids. They were not always pleased by this interest of hers. On the other hand, it did work well for Miss MacManus. She located a suitor for herself and became the wife of John J. Eastland, a maitre d'hôtel at the Hotel.

One of her more exciting moments involved the valet shop. Traditionally, housemen and maintenance men gathered in the valet shop at lunchtime to play cards. As the game progressed, each day "Mom Mom" would interrupt and give special assignments to the housemen to be taken care of at once. In an effort to put a stop to this practice, the valet tied a mouse to the door handle and sure enough, without looking first, she placed her hand on the mouse. She screamed, the mouse escaped, and the card game was never interrupted again. Someone reported later that the mouse, very frightened, was seen in the dining room.

During her thirty-six years of service her fondest recollection would be watching Wilmington come of age. She was a great lady, a hallmark of excellence in her profession.

In 1913, the valet shop was a very active operation in the Housekeeping Department. It was equipped with two eighteen-pound electric irons, two colors of thread (black and white), very few buttons, and only one needle, issued one at a time by the executive housekeeper. Should a button be needed, one simply was cut from a garment already hanging on the rack. Work schedules did not exist; the men cleaned and pressed whenever the guests required service. A bottle was kept in the valet's desk for the reported purpose of recharging body and soul.

John A. Akehurst was the first valet. He joined the staff in September 1913. Jack was born in Surrey, England. Much of his knowledge was gained at the old Waldorf-Astoria in New York. He was considered an outstanding valet and later would become the valet at the Hotel Astor in New York. Jack commented, "I came to Wilmington just to open the valet shop and then meant to return to New York City. However, I found Wilmington and the Hotel du Pont to my liking and remained for thirty-eight years." During this long service, he would train the present valet supervisor, Val Casalena, a Wilmingtonian. For Val, working and training with Jack were among his fondest experiences.

As retirement approached for Mrs. Eastland, a replacement was needed. After a discussion with management, she was allowed to recommend her successor. "A number of years ago a lady came to see me bringing with her a young girl who had been raised on a farm near Middletown, Delaware. Knowing that persons raised on a farm are likely to understand hard work and be dependable, I employed this young lady who was about nineteen years old. She would be assigned the duties of a maid and live in the Hotel. Her name was Mildred Morris. Later, Mildred would marry a member of the Housekeeping Department named John Pierce. I recommended that Mildred be my replacement."

For Mildred this was one of her finest moments: to come from the country for a modest job and then become the executive housekeeper for the Hotel du Pont. One of her unforgettable experiences occurred during the Depression when room occupancy was very low. Mrs. Eastland called Mildred and asked if she would take two weeks off without pay, since she could go home to the farm and so have plenty of food. She explained that many maids were not so fortunate. Mildred was amazed at her thoughtfulness. This is how employees made it through those difficult days.

As the second executive housekeeper, Mrs. Pierce was quickly identified by the employees as the warden. She objected to such a name. Her only self-admitted fault was that she did talk loudly and long.

During her administration Mrs. Pierce would experience two upheavals. First, numerous method men and industrial engineers would make studies concerning operating techniques for equipment, location of furniture, items used, and how to make up a bed and clean a room. Her comments were, "Can you tell me what in the world these fellows, and they were nice, could tell us about how to maintain a bedroom? Why, some of these maids were old enough to be their mothers. Some called me old-fashioned. We did make some changes as a result of their studies. I guess I was not very helpful, and that was wrong. It

was not really a problem." Second, a decision was made to replace all the furniture in the bedrooms. The brass beds, never
lacquered, with a beautiful patina; the bed tables, dressers, and
desks, all mahogany, each top covered with glass (under the
glass would be imported linen, carefully centered, with the Hotel du Pont crest); lovely brass lamps: all of these were to be
replaced. "I would never see this quality again. I still have two
of the lamps. You could purchase these items for very little
money."

An innovation during her administration was the arrival of
new fabrics never heard of before. A suite was furnished in a
new one and was called the "Nylon Suite," which attracted
out-of-state attention and interest. "It was exciting for me and
the maids to see many colors. We had worked with white linens
for years." Many improvements and changes would be made
in the material before it would become widely available. Today,
nylon is a household word.

"Working with the finest group of maids in the world was
most important. Their classification would be changed from
maids to housekeepers, which properly reflected their duties.
My forty years with the Hotel du Pont was a wonderful experience for me." And indeed it was for the Hotel.

An interview with the present executive housekeeper, Lau-
rel P. Smith, may give some more insights into this complex
and responsible position. Mrs. Smith joined the Hotel staff in
April 1968 as a room clerk-cashier. She was later promoted to
assistant executive housekeeper and then to executive housekeeper in March 1973.

Q. What staff is required to provide service for 278 guest
rooms occupied by 95,000 guests per year?

A. Twenty housekeepers, four room inspectresses, ten
housemen, one tailor-valet, three seamstresses, one maintenance technician (part-time employees used for backup: ten
housekeepers, seven housemen).

Q. What is your most important responsibility concerning
employees?

A Training and retraining to maintain the highest standards.

Q. Do housekeepers receive many gratuities?

A. No.

Q. Is the Housekeeping Department computerized?

A. Yes. Computers are necessary for prompt and efficient guest service.

Q. How many pounds of laundry are washed each year?

A. Nearly 500,550 pounds, excluding hand towels and washcloths. This represents an enormous number of items: 15,000 shirts, 12,000 pieces of underwear, and 24,000 socks, handkerchiefs, and the like. This doesn't count the dry cleaning every year: 40,000 suits, 1,800 jackets, 38,000 pairs of trousers, and 1,800 dresses.

Q. Do the laundries lose or damage many items?

A. Yes, and it is a disturbing problem that requires constant follow-up. The Hotel purchases the finest quality in all products. It may become necessary again to wash our own laundry.

Q. How much backup linen is required for each room?

A. Four sets.

Q. Do guests take many items?

A. Yes, mostly terrycloth articles such as towels. The housekeepers call this stealing in small quantities.

Q. Do guests ever abuse the rooms or furniture?

A. It is our experience that occasional damage does take place; however, overall we find guests do respect a beautifully decorated room, particularly one that is well maintained.

Q. How many items will the valet shop clean each year?

A. For just one example, 27,500 items used by employees.

Q. How much soap is used each year?

A. 87,500 cakes.

Q. How many items are selected for each guest room?

A. Approximately seventy specific items must be provided. A committee reviews these items on a regular basis to determine guest acceptance.

Q. What are some of the special requests you receive from the guest?

A. Guests who wish to be roomed on lower floors; requests concerning allergies; pillow problems (many guests bring their own pillows, usually small). Most important are calls received from mothers whose child has left his favorite blanket or toy; there will be no sleep for child or parent until the rescue is effected.

Q. Any others?

A. Many guests believe the manager keeps in reserve bedrooms and tables in the dining rooms for special guests. The policy of the Hotel du Pont is not to set aside facilities for such use, although it is very difficult to convince some guests of this.

Q. Would you discuss the lost and found problems?

A. Some of the items that guests forget include: travel tickets; clocks; umbrellas, men's and women's in sufficient numbers to support a rainout; glasses for reading; sleep blinds; books, paperbacks on love and sex, and intellectual novels; underwear, men's and women's in all sizes and colors, bras in unique designs, colors, and sizes; nighties, tops, bottoms, and gowns in unbelievable colors; toothbrushes and paste in great quantities; cosmetics, men's and women's adequate for a small drugstore; shoes, socks, and panty hose; handkerchiefs, ties, shirts, pants, slacks; costume jewelry; razors, and more.

Half of these items are returned to the guest. The rest are kept for ninety days and, if not called for, are given to the housekeeper. Items of considerable value are placed in a safety deposit box for six months or more. Nearly all such items finally are returned to the guest. One of the great mysteries is why all raincoats reported lost are new London Fogs, and why every shirt claimed to be damaged by the laundry is new and handmade in Hong Kong.

The housekeepers wonder why guests attempt to hide money, jewelry, and other items of value in their rooms, or place money under a pillow or between mattresses. For some reason, *Playboy* and similar but less sophisticated magazines find their way beneath the mattress. Safety deposit boxes are available at no cost to secure each guest's personal valuables.

Q. What is your most pleasant experience?

A. My association with the Hotel du Pont staff. We all help each other. Also, guests' comments regarding the good performance of the housekeepers.

# Room Inspection: Then and Now

From the very beginning, a minimum of one room inspection was made weekly by the general manager, the resident manager, and the executive housekeeper. During such an inspection in 1913, they would examine in each room the patina on the brass bed, the polishing of the sterling silver dresser set and the brass lamps (even the brass cuspidor), the button hook and the pin cushion wrapped in white linen; each item to be repaired would be counted; all of the mahogany furniture would be checked for damage and care. The linen underliners for the glass covering the tops of the furniture would be checked and the embroidered cloths centered. The famous brown blankets must be folded and rolled to display the Hotel crest and placed at the foot of the bed. Nothing was overlooked. The electric fan was checked for noise, then the maid call light, window shades, the carpet and rugs, all made especially for the Hotel. And next the bathroom. Was the lighting bright? The bathtub was solid porcelain, the lavatory of vitreous china; were they spotless? A bathroom always must remind the guest of the freshness of newly fallen snow.

Time passes; new developments, values, and changes arise. What would we find today in a room inspection? Now in the rooms the brass beds and the silver dresser sets are gone, and the fans have been replaced by air conditioning. The bedroom furniture is made by Henkel-Harris, who does not manufacture its beautiful furniture for any other hotel in America. Many antiques reflecting warmth and their own special character are appropriately placed. Original paintings lend a homelike atmosphere. The amenities today include telephones, color televisions, AM and FM radios, wake-up clock radios, short-wave radios for international visitors to listen to broadcasts from their native country, night lights, and king and queen size beds. The bathrooms, finished in Corian®, offer shower caps, retractable drying cords, shampoo, a selection of soaps, mouthwash, and shoe horns. Room information appears in five languages. At night, mints and turn-down service are provided for every room. All this reflects a hallmark of the Hotel du Pont's concern and care for the guest.

# Employee Safety

Safety is imperative, health is essential to happiness, and efficiency is the quality most valuable in an employee. Each is dependent on the others.[1]

The year was 1802. A meeting was called by E. I. du Pont de Nemours, the founder of the Du Pont Company, for two purposes: to announce and divulge the plans for gunpowder mills to be built on the banks of the Brandywine River near Wilmington and to determine a wise policy of fundamental safety for the employees. Had we been present, we would have heard a variety of dialects, predominantly French, with lively Irish and English. We would have understood that this was to be a new venture for the new company and indeed for young America. We also would have understood that the product to be manufactured, black powder, was by nature extremely hazardous. Fully realizing this danger, all of the men present at that meeting made a commitment to safety, a policy which was to continue for themselves and for their families as a way of life and as protection for the community as well, wherever the Du Pont Company ventured.

[1] From a booklet given in 1915 to all employees of the Du Pont Company, *Safety, Health, Efficiency* (Wilmington: E. I. du Pont de Nemours Powder Co., 1915), p. 3.

The impact of this commitment can be felt now by every employee of the Du Pont Company, and it has proved to be a most valuable asset for the firm. Little did those men at that early meeting comprehend the scope of the policy established. Mr. du Pont explained to them that in order to have mills, financing, markets, and healthy employees, with a product such as theirs, the new safety commitment must receive the highest priority. These men were deeply impressed by Mr. du Pont's interest in their safety and that of their families.

To fully realize the extent of this commitment and its survival, one only need visit the Hagley Foundation on the Brandywine where the old powder mills still stand. Above them up the hill is the house built by Mr. du Pont for his own family, so they might share the hazards of the job with the employees.

The basic philosophy that prevails at the Du Pont Company has set a standard of excellence for all industry. The company believes that all accidents and injuries can be prevented. An unsafe employee is an unsatisfactory employee; a manager who cannot provide leadership in safety is an unsatisfactory manager. What are the results? From the National Safety Council comes the fact that the Du Pont Company is sixteen times safer than the chemical industry as a whole and fifty-two times safer than all other American industry combined.

This early tradition made a profound influence when, in 1911, plans were made for the Hotel to be owned and operated by the company. In the excitement of formulating and selecting designs and construction, the old dedication to safety was not forgotten.

During the process of construction and in all later expansions, every known safety feature was incorporated to comply with long established safety rules and regulations. These standards in most cases exceeded even those set forth by the local city and state building codes.

What have been the results at the Hotel du Pont? The Hotel holds the World Safety Record (Service Industries classification) of the National Safety Council. This means that the employees of the Hotel du Pont have worked for nine years, or over five million hours, without a lost-time injury on the job. This accomplishment and twenty-four other major awards since 1943 clearly demonstrate that the employees of the Hotel can and do work safely.

# Procedures to Safeguard Food

The director of the General Services Department called a meeting in 1953 to discuss and investigate the procedures followed by the Hotel to prevent food poisoning. Two basic questions were set forth: What causes food contamination? How can it be prevented? To answer these questions, members of the medical profession, the State Board of Health, the Food and Drug Administration of the U.S. Department of Health, and members of the Hotel staff all were involved.

As studies moved forward, it was determined that the medical profession was concerned primarily with the treatment of those made ill due to food poisoning. The State Board of Health, while willing to conduct inspections, was not properly staffed to answer effectively the many questions which arose. A report made to Congress by the Food and Drug Administration indicated that its support in the field of food sanitation was largely ineffective. While the food handlers of the Hotel and those responsible were deeply concerned for safety procedures in the preparation of food, more information was needed.

Responsibilities were assigned at once to begin developing answers to the basic questions of cause and prevention. The managers recognized that there would be frustrations in the

Hotel, a new mode of operation for food handlers, and more; on the other hand, they understood that this project must receive the highest priority.

The first question, what causes food poisoning? Little information was available. As the study went forward, facts began to fall into place, and in analyzing what information was available it was found that five specific areas must be examined for their impact on food sanitation. These areas came under the heading of biological/bacterial contamination. Further studies revealed that eighty percent of the illnesses reported fell in the category of staphyloccocal. It was then necessary to determine symptoms, causative agents, foods involved, the source of bacteria, and control measures. It was found that these bacteria grow with or without oxygen at 45°–115°F, survive wide temperature ranges, and thrive in moist, high-protein foods; they give off a toxin, the culprit that causes illness. Boiling does not kill this toxin, which has no odor.

With these facts and more at hand, the second question was asked, how can it be prevented? Some of the early problems were created unknowingly by the employees and the supervision of the Hotel, who were conscientious and concerned and certainly did not want to cause any illness. Some thought that a clean, shiny preparation area alone was the answer; it is not. Others worried about production control, food costs, and so on. The new program of procedures meant a new day and a new way of life for all employees, and those failing to embrace these procedures would have their jobs in jeopardy. A disciplinary program of reprimand, probation, and termination was initiated for violations.

Three years' exhaustive work on the part of a great number of people, and in particular by Dr. Ben Hodge, medical supervisor for the General Services Department, resulted in the following procedures to prevent food poisoning:

- Areas of responsibility established for all members of supervision;
- Communications, both oral and written;

- Training programs for all food handlers: frequency and scope;
- Inspection procedures and what was to be covered;
- Selection and training of a food sanitarian;
- Follow-up written tests for all employees;
- Examination of food specifications, including those involving the vendors;
- Examination of areas beyond the Hotel, such as inspections of food-processing plants (our visits are welcomed) and checks of temperature in refrigerated trucks;
  - Meetings for reviewing all programs;
  - Orientation for new food handlers;
  - A complete food procedures manual, covering the procedures necessary to prevent food poisoning, which would become the "How Manual" for all;
  - Arrangements with the Quality Control Laboratory in Philadelphia. This laboratory is approved by the Food and Drug Administration. No specifications or time limits would be established without the knowledge of the laboratory.

What have been the results?

The State Board of Health looks upon the Hotel as a training ground for new sanitarians. A minimum of two formal inspections is conducted by the board during the year. The Hotel receives about seven violations out of a possible 113, and eighteen demerits out of a possible 200. These low figures indeed are a remarkable performance.

Visits are also made by representatives of the Food and Drug Administration. The classification of the Hotel by this agency is "excellent." Only two percent of the 350,000 food facilities in the United States preparing and serving food to the public receive such a rating. A demerit score must be under twenty of 300 violations to be considered excellent. Representatives of the Food and Drug Administration consider the Hotel's program, and particularly the food procedures manual, to be the finest of its type in this country. This same agency has asked permission of the Hotel to use the manual in national training programs.

The Hotel is proud of its accomplishments in one of the most important phases of its responsibilities: to safeguard the guests and employees from food related illnesses. Management fully recognizes that day to day follow-up and constant vigilance are necessary for an effective and successful program.

# Names of Rooms

Guests often ask, how were the names for the Hotel's public and private facilities selected? There are as many answers to this question as there are names. In most cases, sufficient thought is not given by those who suggest names and those who approve them. During the history of the Hotel du Pont, many names have been given to rooms, and many have been changed. We will share with you why and how the present names were selected. Here are the basics used as a guide: relationship to the property, meaningfulness, ease in pronouncing and remembering, and clarity for the guest. Naming a facility for a living person is very complex and usually has been avoided.

### HOTEL DU PONT

The Du Pont Company approved the project to build the Hotel in 1912 and provided the financial backing. At that time, the Hotel Du Pont Co. was incorporated to administer the property. Later, the Hotel Du Pont Co. was dissolved in 1934 and all assets, except cash, were sold to the Du Pont Building Corp. No other hotel would bear the name Du Pont.

### GREEN ROOM

It was the custom during 1913 to identify the principal, and in most cases the only, dining room as the Main Dining Room. As the Hotel added other dining facilities, that name became confusing to the guests. It was renamed the Green Room, which has become legend and known around the world.

How was this name selected? There are several versions. The green room is an area in a theater or concert hall where actors or entertainers relax before or between or after a performance; it appears that this definition or meaning was overlooked during the selection process. Another version, with very little to support it, is that the decor of the room at that time was largely green. Should that have been important, what would happen to the name should the color scheme be changed? Another story stems from the fact that Mr. and Mrs. John J. Raskob, during this period, maintained a suite in the Hotel. Mr. Raskob at that time was secretary-treasurer of the Hotel Du Pont Co., and Mrs. Raskob's maiden name was Helena Springer Green. Could that have had an influence? While no written documentation has been supplied to support this conclusion, many accept this version.

During a study to evaluate names of the facilities, the Green Room came under discussion, and the decision was reached to recommend that the Green Room's name be changed to the Delaware Room. Many good reasons were offered in support of the name change, as well as many objections. The change was recommended and approved, but on the next day the manager's wife did not agree. The manager asked for the action to be suspended. In all probability, the guests too did not want any changes in the Green Room, not even in its name.

### GRILLE

This term often is used by many hotels for an informal restaurant, or rathskeller, located in this instance on the lower level. Many of the services, such as music for nightly dancing, provided by this room filled a social need in the early days of the Hotel. To this day, many Delawareans have fond memories and a special place in their hearts for the old Grille.

### BRANDYWINE ROOM

The Du Pont Company started its business enterprise in 1802 with gunpowder mills on the banks of the Brandywine River, just outside Wilmington. The river was named by Swedish settlers who had landed in Wilmington in 1638. Its historic relationship to the Hotel and community is meaningful and beautiful.

### CHRISTINA ROOM

The Christina River flows into the Brandywine and was named by the early settlers for their queen in Sweden. During Wilmington's early history, the primary port for trade and commerce was located on this river. Inns and taverns of that day were built within a few blocks of this port. Today the Brandywine and Christina Rooms flow together like the rivers they are named for.

### GOLD BALLROOM

The requirements in 1917 of Pierre S. du Pont for the proposed new ballroom were threefold: it would be one of the largest and most magnificent ballrooms in America and, possibly, in the world; architecturally, it would tell a story; stylistically, it would be in the Louis XVI period, decorated in gold and embellished by walls executed in the rare technique of sgraffito. The lavish use of gold in the designs inspired the name.

### DU BARRY ROOM

Why the name du Barry? Madame du Barry (1743–1793), née Marie Jeanne Bécu, was a famous beauty and the mistress of Louis XV of France, with great power at Court. She disgraced many powerful ministers and during the French Revolution was accused of cooperating against the new Republic; she was beheaded in 1793. There are no documents to support the conclusion that the room was named for her, although the du Barry Room is lovely, and the architecture is of the same period as her reign. Her profile is on one of the medallions of famous beauties in the Gold Ballroom.

There is a Du Pont connection with the lady, which Pierre S. du Pont may or may not have known in 1913. His ancestor, Pierre Samuel du Pont de Nemours, who was the progenitor of the Delaware Du Ponts and the father of E. I., the powder maker, knew the young Jeanne in his youth. She was a member of a drawing class in which his sister was enrolled and for which he sometimes posed. He noted with some regret in his autobiography that he was "not among the numerous predecessors of King Louis XV."[2]

### PRIVATE DINING ROOMS

These rooms, during the opening in 1913, were referred to as parlors and identified by letters of the alphabet. Today, with the exception of two suites, the rooms are named for our state, counties, and several cities. The Delaware Suite is located on the eleventh floor overlooking the Delaware River and the site where the Swedes landed. Other rooms, on the second floor, are named Dover, for the capital; New Castle, Kent, and Sussex, for the three counties; and Georgetown, Seaford, and Yorklyn. All of them are meaningful to Delawareans.

### BEDROOM SUITES

Many years ago, Pierre S. du Pont received a letter from the manager which covered two points: the Hotel was planning to renovate his suite; they planned to name it the Longwood Suite after his country estate and would appreciate his thoughts and ideas concerning the decoration. In most cases Mr. du Pont

[2] Ambrose Saricks, *Pierre Samuel du Pont de Nemours* (Lawrence, Kansas: The University of Kansas Press, 1965), p. 14.

answered such memos in writing, but in this case he tele-
phoned. "I have received your letter concerning your plans for
my suite, and I am not of the opinion it needs redecorating
and, under no condition, will it be named Longwood. I would
appreciate it if the whole matter was placed in abeyance." A
letter to Mr. du Pont assured him no further action would be
considered.

Today, a few suites are named, such as the Honeymoon,
Governor's, Mayor's, International, Ambassador's, and General
Manager's Suites. Many guests feel honored to be assigned
these rooms, and they are very much in demand. The bellmen
and housekeepers enjoy namedropping and talking with guests
about these suites. "Tonight you will occupy the room Lindbergh stayed in," or "This is the room the late P. S. du Pont
occupied." The guests love such information and frequently ask
employees to name dignitaries and point out their rooms. The
answers may not always be accurate, but one fact is sure:
hundreds of celebrities and dignitaries have stayed in the Hotel
du Pont over the years.

# Architects and Designers

When the Hotel du Pont opened to the public in 1913, it was considered a master achievement in hotel architecture and ingenuity.

The architectural decoration of the Hotel reflects a great tradition dating from the era when the skilled craftmanship of woodcarvers, painters, and stonemasons and varying ornamental techniques were still available to architects and designers to richly embellish walls, ceilings, doors, and passageways. The artists and craftsmen who executed these designs were trained and steeped in the traditions and techniques of period ornamentation and today, for the most part, have vanished with the guild systems here and abroad.

This story would not be complete without setting forth the names of the ladies and gentlemen who designed and executed the classic and sophisticated work that has been called beautiful, magnificent, truly elegant: the Hotel du Pont.

FREDERICK GODLEY, J. ANDRÉ FOUILHOUX, AND JOEL BARBER, NEW YORK

These were the principal architects during the construction of the Hotel.

### RAYMOND M. HOOD, NEW YORK

Mr. Hood's primary accomplishments were the design of the Lobby, Gold Ballroom, du Barry Room, and Grille. The four oval figures, or cartouches, in the corners of the Ballroom and the ceiling in this room were his design. The work was executed by M. R. Giusti, an architectural modeler. Later in his career, Mr. Hood was the architect for the Chicago *Tribune* Tower and a consultant to the Rockefeller Center complex.

### RENÉ CHAMBELLAN, NEW YORK

The gnomes in the Grille were designed by Mr. Hood and executed by Mr. Chambellan. His expertness in modeling was also used in rooms for the Board of Directors and the Executive Committee and on the elevator doors in the Lobby.

### VIOLET TERWILLIGER, NEW YORK

Miss Terwilliger designed and sculpted the medallions of the twenty famous beauties of history and literature in the Gold Ballroom. She also did the panels at the springing line and the octagonal panels near the base in that room.

### DUNCAN SMITH, NEW YORK

Mr. Smith designed and executed the sgraffito work in the Gold Ballroom.

### DOMENICO MORTELLITO, NEW YORK AND WILMINGTON

His many contributions as an artist, designer, and consultant on the interiors of the Hotel include the preservation of the Green Room's original design, the mural decoration in the stairway and foyer to the Grille, and the murals for the Nemours Soda Shop.

### EDWARD C. MAY, JR., WILMINGTON

Mr. May, an architect with the Du Pont Company's General Services Department, has been involved in the design and execution of the designs involving renovations for many years. Mrs. Joanne Seybold Hastings was employed by the Hotel in 1947 as an interior decorator. She later joined Mr. May and continued as a consultant to the Hotel. Mrs. Alice Carter Breger now has assumed this responsibility.

### ROBERT M. ENGELBRECHT, NEW YORK

Mr. Engelbrecht designed the Lobby and bedroom furnishings in 1961.

### CLIFF YOUNG, NEW YORK

A nationally known designer and muralist, Mr. Young was responsible for the restoration and repair of the Italian sgraffito handwork on the walls of the Gold Ballroom. Mr. Young was referred to the Hotel by the Metropolitan Museum of Art in New York. He was one of the few muralists who knew this intricate process.

### WALTER M. BALLARD, NEW YORK

This company was the principal designer of hotels during the years 1964 to 1980. Its work includes the food preparation areas, public and private dining rooms, cocktail lounges, Gold Ballroom, du Barry Room, and the Nemours Soda Shop. The designs were executed by the Office Buildings Division of the General Services Department.

### OTHERS

Highly regarded architects were called by management as consultants on specific questions. Among these were Morris Whiteside and William Moeckel of the Wilmington firm of Whiteside, Moeckel, and Carbonell; Stanley White, a New York architect; and Charles Keck, a sculptor from New York. Input from all levels of management in the Du Pont Company was of considerable importance and contributed greatly to the decisions concerning final designs and execution. The Hotel du Pont is a living example of the talents of these outstanding professionals.

The Brandywine
Room in 1941 . . .

. . . in 1954

. . . in 1967

# Unusual Roles

# Nemours Soda Shop

The Nemours Soda Shop is named for the office building in which it is located, across from the Du Pont Building in Wilmington. While sodas may be obtained, it is primarily a modified lunchroom. All service is provided by stand up counters and two take out stations, except for a few tables.

Most of its patrons are Du Pont Company employees. A number have not changed their order for lunch in years. Lloyd Taylor, director of the Advertising Department of the Du Pont Company, once commented about the operation, "I have been eating in the Soda Shop off and on for twenty years, and the only change I've seen on the menu board is the price increase." As a result, a small menu board now offers a daily special.

More Du Pont Company executives can be found at lunchtime waiting in line and standing at these counters than in any other Hotel facility. The counter service waitresses, who know and are known by a large number of the executives, enjoy an employee training of sorts by advising an executive on what should be changed within the company. As the executive departs, the employee is sometimes asked if she knows the person just spoken to. As she finds out, you might hear her say, "I hope he does not remember me or what I said." The executives

175

enjoy the food and pleasant experience during the brief lunch period.

Should you ask the patrons who have been using this room for years what impresses them most, some would say the waitresses, some the variety of soups and sandwiches, and some the mural they look at each day. When the decorations for the Soda Shop were first discussed, it was assumed that they would depict some local or historic scene, such as the Battle of the Brandywine. Instead, based upon the fact that this was a place for stand up lunches and the patrons needed some visual entertainment while they were eating, it was decided to provide a design which would be cheerful and amusing.

The artist developed the concept of double imaged vegetables. The subject was not only appropriate for an eatery but provided rich colors. The technique used was carved lacquered linoleum. The subjects were first carved in battleship linoleum, which is twice as thick as any linoleum made today. They were then painted with lacquers and polished with floor polishing machines. The medium has withstood exposure to cooking vapors and steam tables these many years.

The subject matter is delightful because, in the double imaged vegetables, we find among others that the stalk of celery becomes a ballet dancer, the squash a duck, the peas a wood nymph, the grape leaf a frog, the loaf of bread and frankfurter roll a chef, the pepper an elephant, the ear of corn a horse, and the little radish lying lazily on its back the artist at work, Domenico Mortellito.

The panel at the far end of the Soda Shop depicts the four basic meats: beef, which is a composite of a pear and a peach, cut in half; lamb, an eggplant and a head of cauliflower; pork, a tomato; and poultry, a banana and raspberries. Here again the murals are done in keeping with the basic design and scale of the room. The carved lacquered linoleum provides an interesting juxtaposition of color, texture, and pattern to go with the other materials and textures in the Soda Shop. This is an extraordinary setting for a quick stand up lunch.

# The Cafeterias

### THE GRILL CAFETERIA

The little grotesques, or gnomes, located at the top of the high oak columns have watched over the Grille since the gala opening of the Hotel in 1913. Many Delawareans have lasting and pleasant memories of evenings in this room. Should you mention the Hotel du Pont in Delaware, their immediate response is, "We will always remember the Grille." Just the other day a retired executive stopped by to have lunch with friends and remarked, "I have just completed a refinishing job on a table and four chairs, custom made of oak, which were purchased for the Grille in 1913. They are just beautiful and remind me of many happy nights I spent in this room. I think I paid $1.25 for each one. Those were the days!"

Many changes have taken place over the years. With the passage of the Prohibition Act in 1920, service in the room was restricted to lunch only. In 1933, when the act was repealed, the Grille again became a popular nightclub. In 1949, after World War II, the room was discontinued as a restaurant and cocktail lounge. It reopened in 1951 as a public cafeteria, renamed "The Grill." At the same time, the Hotel's employee cafeteria was discontinued.

Now on weekdays cafeteria service is provided for breakfast and lunch, followed by table service for dinner. Early in the morning, corporate executives, many business leaders of the community, and employees line up to purchase freshly baked pastries and coffee for an office treat later. One young lady was heard to say, "Why, it's a conglomeration of lovely people." The Grill is also used for social affairs on weekends and holidays.

The service provided over the years has changed, and re-decorations have taken many directions. However, the room's effectiveness to the company and community is constant. On occasion, as you leave the Grill, you may hear the gnomes say, "Do you think sometime they will return our room to its glory of yesteryear?"

### THE LOUVIERS CAFETERIA

In 1952, this cafeteria was opened as a private facility to serve lunch only to employees of the Engineering Department, which had transferred from Wilmington to the Louviers Building. This building is located near Newark, Delaware, fourteen miles from Wilmington in beautiful rolling countryside. While it is a company cafeteria, visitors to the site are welcome. The location of the dining room makes it possible for the employees to view the flowering dogwood and shrubs in the spring and the lovely landscaped lawn all summer. During the winter when it snows, the hills appear as a winter wonderland.

The production and service equipment is complete in every detail. With one or two exceptions, all cafeteria employees work twenty hours a week, which qualifies them for Du Pont Company benefits. The employees of the Engineering Department are fortunate to have so many local and helpful people to care for their dining needs. The conversation along the service line is chatty and homelike; however it may, on occasion, slow the line to a stop. The Hotel is proud to be a part of this operation.

### THE EXPERIMENTAL STATION CAFETERIA

This cafeteria is a part of history and was built in 1924. It is a stone's throw from the Brandywine River, not far from the Du Pont Company's first black powder mills on the opposite shore. The building was used originally as the clubhouse for the Du Pont Country Club. The club expanded and moved across the road many years ago, and now extensive research laboratories for the Du Pont Company's Experimental Station surround the old clubhouse. As on other company sites, the cafeteria is private for the use of employees.

The staff of the cafeteria in all probability receives more scientific comments and directions than any cafeteria in the country. No aspect of food service is overlooked by the patrons. An understanding and meaningful language has developed between the chemists and the cafeteria workers. This assignment is special for Hotel employees, and they always enjoy it.

# The Vending Operation

On the horizon of American business, there came into being what is now known as the coffee break. Employees of the Du Pont Company quickly adopted this new concept of fifteen minutes in the morning and afternoon. Great numbers of employees descended upon the Grill and Nemours Soda Shop during their breaks. The Hotel was not prepared to serve effectively such large numbers. Fifteen minutes in many cases became thirty minutes or longer, which was not satisfactory to either the employees or management. As the company expanded, this problem became even more accute. A study was authorized in 1960 to examine the matter and recommend alternatives.

Accordingly, in February 1961 coffee carts were initiated to provide service on each floor. Time schedules and the location of such a service were communicated throughout the buildings. These carts became known as little rolling restaurants, and while they were a time-saving improvement, three problems arose: they were heavy, too large for passenger elevators, and awkward for one person to maneuver. Their appearance and the little bell that sounded their arrival hardly were in keeping with what you might expect in the executive headquarters. Investigations continued to determine the direction of such service. In April 1968, test installations of vending machines started in the Nemours Building. While this service did not enjoy a very good reputation, it was an improvement over the carts.

During the next three years, the vending service was expanded. Machines became more sophisticated and dependable. In 1972 the carts were discontinued, and locations for vending were determined for the Du Pont and Nemours Buildings. Today the vending areas are beautifully designed and blend into the architecture of the buildings. The planning for the new Brandywine Building in Wilmington particularly included suitable locations for such service.

A few statistics may be of interest. Machines prepare 160 gallons of coffee in the morning and again in the afternoon. During the year, 344,000 cold drinks, 107,000 cups of tea and Sanka, 30,000 sandwiches, 141,000 snacks and candy, and 17,280 pounds of coffee appear from 230 machines. Menu planning is important, and over 300 items are rotated during the year. Nearly 12,000 employees use this food service, now available during all hours. The operation is managed professionally and receives the same attention as any other food department.

*Waiting . . .*

*Crossroads*

# A Major Decision (1955)

The Du Pont Company in 1955 rethought and examined its hotel requirements in Wilmington and the whole future of the Hotel du Pont. The question had been on the minds of company executives for several years: Should the Hotel be continued or closed? Much information was needed by the Executive Committee to find the answer. Studies were categorized into Du Pont's Wilmington hotel needs and the future of the Hotel; a financial analysis of the Hotel; the public relations aspects; input by department heads; and needs and cost to modernize and bring the Hotel up to date. To reestablish the Hotel du Pont as a first class property would involve twelve projects costing $5 million.[1]

To determine the company's requirements, hotel facilities were divided into four main categories: rooms; private functions; first class dining; and mass feeding facilities. As a result of the study, the company concluded that there was a substantial need for hotel facilities which could be met by building a modern first class hotel within a few blocks of 10th and Market Streets. It followed that construction of a new hotel would not be financially attractive unless the Hotel du Pont closed.

[1] Report to the Executive Committee by the General Services Department, February 17, 1955.

The Grill Cafeteria and Nemours Soda Shop appeared to be necessary adjuncts to the office buildings and were not a normal function of a hotel. Therefore, the operation of these facilities in their present locations should persist and not be contingent upon the continued operation of the Hotel.[2]

The most attractive plan to the company at that stage was to discontinue hotel operations, with which they had never been comfortable, and convert to offices. But points were raised which made them pause.

First, it did not seem feasible to get out of the food business entirely; present plans called for the retention of the Grill and Nemours Soda Shop. The executive dining rooms and a large function room would be retained for company use. Second, the convenience of having a good restaurant and hotel as part of the office buildings complex was well recognized by company employees, customers, and suppliers alike. The assurance of high quality food, properly prepared and served, and the control of hotel rooms were advantages of value which could not be measured in terms of dollars. And third, public relations were one of the strongest reasons for getting out of the hotel business, a possible source of adverse publicity for the company. The exposure which the company incurred in its hotel, and which was out of all proportion to the significance of such an operation to a chemical company, would be eliminated. On the other hand, closing the Hotel would have a major and negative impact on relations with employees and the Wilmington public in general, who had enjoyed the Hotel in the midst of its community for over forty years.

Other alternatives were to enter into negotiations with local investors to examine the discontinuance of most of the Hotel's facilities in favor of a new hotel to be built nearby at 9th and Shipley Streets; to discuss with hotel chains such as Hilton,

[2] Ibid., July 18, 1955.

Statler, and other first class operations their interest in building a hotel in Wilmington; and to approve the proposed project and continue to operate the Hotel as a facility of the company.

Studies and discussions of this magnitude could not be kept confidential. The possible closing was the overwhelming concern of the four hundred Hotel employees. Many of the long-service employees said, "I bet if Mr. Pierre were alive, no study would be made." Other employees were in total disbelief: why, what would Wilmington be like without the Hotel du Pont? Others called on the manager hoping for some reassurance, which he could not give. The community heard rumors and wrote letters and made telephone calls. The studies would go on. Other information was requested; the wait for the decision now began.

Finally, after what appeared to be a very long time, the answer came: the Du Pont Company would continue to operate the Hotel du Pont, and the project was approved. The primary reason for approval was that the need for a first class hotel was just as great in 1955 as it had been in 1913. Whether the Du Pont Company operated a complete hotel facility or not, it concluded that the annual cost to the company for hotel and restaurant accommodations in Wilmington would be essentially the same.

Other decisions and comments made by the Executive Committee at that time would be most helpful to future administrations. Wages and salaries of a general nature were to be increased for Hotel employees when other company departments announced increases, and the amount of the increases should be compared to the wages and salaries paid by other first class hotels. Harris, Kerr, Forster & Co., experts in hotel accounting procedures, were to be employed to select a number of first class transient hotels in the New England and mid-Atlantic states for the purpose of establishing a financial procedure to compare and measure the Hotel du Pont's operating effectiveness. The Hotel was not to be expanded in scope and, while it was understood that the hotel business is a marginal venture for a chemical company, it was not expected to lose any money. This particular and historic decision had a profound and positive effect on the Hotel du Pont's operation for years to come.

While the opening of the Hotel du Pont in January 1913 was one of the most meaningful occasions for the city of Wilmington, the approval to continue operating the Hotel in 1955 would be considered by its employees and the community at large a much greater moment.

# The Present (1981)

This story has not been an attempt to set forth the administration of any particular manager or time period but rather to put in place all that has been a part of the Hotel du Pont's character and personality. It appears desirable to ask an important question as we reflect on the Hotel's performance over these sixty-seven years. Has the Hotel du Pont accomplished the primary objectives set forth in 1911, to serve the needs of the Du Pont Company and the business, civic, and social sectors of the city? Over the years Hotel management has been sensitive to and ever mindful of these aims.

Has the Hotel du Pont served the needs of the Du Pont Company? To answer this question, the management of twenty-three specific departments of the Du Pont Company were called upon by the author to discuss in detail and examine the services provided by the Hotel. The departmental executives were generous and appreciative in their comments about the important contributions made by the Hotel to good customer relations. All of them seemed pleased with "their" Hotel. The corporate position is described best by Irving S. Shapiro, chairman of the board and chief executive officer. "We are proud of the Hotel du Pont. It is of high importance to the company in the area of

180

public affairs." The Public Affairs Department is charged with
the responsibility of examining and appraising the public image
of the company's operations. Information furnished by this department clearly shows that the Hotel du Pont in its sixty-eight
year history has been a meaningful asset to the image of the
company in the broad field of customer relations and to the
community at large.

Has the Hotel over the years served the business, civic, and
social needs of the community? To answer this question, several
hundred letters from guests were examined, reservations covering a period of fifty years were studied, and records of Hotel
sales calls were evaluated. The letters reveal one primary theme:
"We are proud of our Hotel. We have come to expect quality,
atmosphere, a feeling of comfort, and most important, professionalism. It is a classic, an institution in our community. This
is why we come time and time again."

The review of reservations shows that the Hotel has served
the community in all areas and indeed has become, from its
opening, the business, civic, and social center of our city. It is
gratifying to see the many organizations that have enjoyed from
twenty-five to sixty years of association with the Hotel. Service
clubs, fraternal organizations, civic and social groups and businesses have perpetual reservations as far as ten years in advance, a fact which clearly demonstrates the complete trust
and confidence of their members in the Hotel's future.

The Hotel sales office was asked why so many potential
guests visit to arrange tours, small conventions, seminars,
training meetings, and business luncheons. The answer is because of the Hotel's reputation, its beautiful facilities, the good
maintenance, and most important, the pleasant and caring employees. There is an overall feeling of dependability.

William G. Copeland, C.L.U., president of Continental American Life Insurance Co., summarizes it well. "The Hotel is, and
has been, a major institution that directly and indirectly touches
the social and economic fabric of the entire state. Its importance

and contributions continue to increase with the passage of time. The Hotel du Pont is truly a marvelous blend of tradition with progress." This comment is particularly meaningful to the Hotel, for the insurance company arranged one of the first meetings held in the new building in March 1913.

What comment would the seven managers most want to make? (There are but two left). "We are all very proud of the Hotel, and it has been a privilege for us to share in its administration." Each one had his own special influence and made valuable contributions.

The founders who recommended the venture and put it all in place, wherever they are today, are looking in through the picture window, smiling and approving the stewardship over the years since it opened in 1913. Quiet elegance, homelike, attractive in the highest degree: your Hotel.

*Lobby and entrance to the Green Room before and after renovation in 1953*

# Appendix A

## Heads of Departments for the Grand Opening

| Name & Position | Previously Employed | Location |
|---|---|---|
| Ernest S. Taite, Manager | Hotel Astor | New York City |
| S. M. Bullwinkle, Assistant Manager | Hotel Astor | New York City |
| *Miss Margaret T. MacManus, Executive Housekeeper | Hotel Astor | New York City |
| E. Garraux, Executive Chef | Hotel Gotham | New York City |
| J. E. C. Donnelly, Wine Steward | Hotel Astor | New York City |
| *John A. Akehurst, Valet | Hotel Astor | New York City |
| James J. Nolan, Steward | Hotel Arlington | Washington, DC |
| Harry J. Harkins, Room Manager | Clayton House | Wilmington, DE |

*Remained to finish their careers in the Hotel du Pont.

| Name & Position | Previously Employed | Location |
|---|---|---|
| Robert McSorley, Room Clerk | St. James Hotel | Philadelphia, PA |
| Frank Moran, Front Clerk | Continental Hotel | Philadelphia, PA |
| J. J. Hannan, Front Clerk | Waldorf-Astoria | New York City |
| W. H. Whidden, Headwaiter | Grand Hotel | New York City |
| Miss L. Hamer, Front Cashier | Hotel Patten | Chattanooga, TN |
| Miss I. Ross, Front Cashier | Rittenhouse Hotel | Philadelphia, PA |

# Appendix B

*Dinner Menu on Opening Day*

Canapés Assortis
Maurice River Cove Oysters
Tortue Verte Claire à la Fine Champagne
Olives          Celery          Radis
Sea Bass Sauté à la Meunière
Pommes à la Parisienne
Ris de Veau aux Champignons
Poussin Royal Rôti
Salade Excelsior
Glace Fantaisie
Petits Fours

Café Noir

Clysmic Spring Water

# Appendix C

*Press Reviews of Opening Day*

*The Morning News* (Wilmington), January 16, 1913:
 Successful beyond expression was the opening this week of the Hotel du Pont when 25,000 people, conservatively estimated, passed in and out its doors with nothing but praise for the magnificent hostelry. Faces familiar in every walk of Delaware's social, professional, and business life appeared as a part of the new building. It was truly homelike.
 On every side there was praise. Not only were Wilmingtonians represented, but there were hundreds of people from downstate and all parts of the country who visited the Hotel during the day.

*Every Evening* (Wilmington), January 16, 1913:
 The tremendous surprise that greeted the guests when they entered the Hotel du Pont yesterday was well worth the secrecy that management has preserved. The whole building is finished beautifully and the best workmanship was used everywhere. Every detail is worked out carefully and all rooms are most tasteful. The Hotel is a beautifully finished product of the architect and builder's art.

# Appendix D

## HOTEL DU PONT COMPANY MANAGEMENT PERSONNEL (8/14/12 to 6/30/34)

| PRESIDENT | VICE PRESIDENT | SECRETARY | TREASURER | HOTEL MANAGER |
|---|---|---|---|---|
| P. S. du Pont *August 1912–January 1920* | E. S. Taite *August 1912–July 1921* | J. J. Raskob *August 1912–January 1920* | J. J. Raskob *August 1912–January 1920* | E. S. Taite *August 1912–June 1921* |
| F. G. Tallman *January 1920–June 1925* | W. P. Allen *July 1921–November 1921* | Alexis I. du Pont *January 1920–June 1921* | W. F. Raskob *January 1920–June 1934* | H. J. Harkins *June 1921–January 1927* |
| R. R. M. Carpenter *June 1925–June 1929* | J. P. Niles *November 1921–January 1926* | W. F. Raskob *June 1921–July 1921* | | C. W. Gibbs *January 1927–June 1933* |
| W. B. Foster *June 1929–May 1931* | F. S. MacGregor *January 1926–February 1928* | C. Copeland *July 1921–June 1930* | | H. Shreffler (Acting) *June 1933–November 1933* |
| E. M. Taylor *May 1931–June 1934* | E. M. Taylor *February 1928–May 1931* | E. A. Howard *June 1930–June 1934* | | F. C. Gregson *November 1933–May 1953* |
| | W. F. Raskob *May 1931–June 1934* | | | |

On June 30, 1934, the Hotel Du Pont Company was dissolved and its assets (except cash) and liabilities were sold to the Du Pont Building Corporation.

# GENERAL SERVICES DEPARTMENT

## DIRECTOR

E. M. Taylor
*October 1936–July 1941*

F. G. Tallman, Jr.
*July 1941–October 1952*

J. A. Grady
*October 1952–January 1973*

J. C. Stewart
*January 1973–August 1980*

D. L. Longenecker
*August 1980–To Date*

## HOTEL MANAGER

F. C. Gregson
*November 1933–May 1953*

J. D. LaMothe
*May 1953–April 1968*

H. V. Ayres
*April 1968–October 1978*

F. Wieland
*October 1978–To Date*

# HOTEL DU PONT ORGANIZATION CHART

## GENERAL SERVICES DEPARTMENT DIRECTOR

### HOTEL GENERAL MANAGER

- **Food and Beverage Manager**
  - Food Preparation
  - Banquet
  - Dining Rooms
  - Cafeterias
  - Vending

- **Sales Manager**
  - Tour Coordinator

- **Resident Manager**
  - Front Desk
  - Housekeepers
  - Night Auditor

# Appendix E

*Yearly Food Purchases (1979)\**

*Meat*

| | | |
|---|---|---|
| Ribs | 44,300 pounds | |
| Whole Filets | 32,400 pounds | |
| Sirloin | 15,250 pounds | |
| Veal | 6,600 pounds | 128,550 pounds |
| Lamb | 10,300 pounds | |
| Bottom Round | 14,000 pounds | |
| Top Butt | 5,700 pounds | |

*Poultry*

| | | |
|---|---|---|
| Chicken | 61,000 pounds | |
| Ducks | 11,000 pounds | 102,600 pounds |
| Pheasant | 600 pounds | |
| Turkey | 30,000 pounds | |

*Seafood*

| | | |
|---|---|---|
| Fresh Backfin Crabmeat | 10,200 pounds | |
| Lobster Tails | 3,900 pounds | |
| Fresh Lobster | 1,500 pounds | 61,600 pounds |
| Shrimp | 14,000 pounds | |
| Fish | 32,000 pounds | |

\* This list does not include fresh vegetables and fruit and staples.

*Dairy Products*

| | |
|---|---|
| ½ pints White Milk | 45,000 |
| Quarts White Milk | 6,000 |
| ½ pints Skim Milk | 26,160 |
| ½ pints Chocolate Milk | 19,800 |
| ½ pints Buttermilk | 28,400 |
| Quarts Light Cream | 900 |
| Quarts Heavy Cream | 22,600 |
| Pounds Cottage Cheese | 8,940 |
| Quarts Coffee Cream | 38,000 |
| Dozens of Eggs | 33,000 |

*Other*

| | |
|---|---|
| Sugar 6X | 14,400 pounds |
| Brown Sugar | 7,200 pounds |
| Granulated Sugar | 60,000 pounds |
| All Purpose Flour | 110,000 pounds |
| Hi Gluten | 54,000 pounds |
| Misc. Flour (Rye, Wheat, Etc.) | 80,000 pounds |
| Coffee (excluding Vending Operation) | 17,500 pounds |
| Sanka (excluding Vending Operation) | 400 pounds |

TOTAL FOOD PURCHASED                $2,160,000

TOTAL WINE AND LIQUOR PURCHASED        $290,000

# Appendix F

*Weekly Average Bake Shop Production (1979)*

| | |
|---:|---|
| 1,700 | loaves of bread |
| 1,700 | dozens of assorted rolls |
| 1,100 | dozens of Danish pastry |
| 450 | 10″ cakes |
| 475 | 8″ pies |
| 725 | dozens of muffins |
| 650 | pounds of macaroons |
| 100 | pounds of assorted cookies |
| 4,000 | French pastries |
| 750 | napoleons |
| 5,200 | small quiches Lorraine (cocktail party style) |
| 2,000 | profiteroles |
| 28 | gallons of pancake mix |
| 75 | casata |
| 75 | apple strudels |
| 600 | tart and seafood shells |
| 16 | gallons of ice cream |
| 10 | gallons of sherbet |
| 300 | cup custards |
| 700 | baked alaskas |

# Appendix G

## *Modernization Program (1955–1958)*

*Exterior Modernization*
Replace Terra-Cotta Ornamentation
Steam Clean Base Tier
Replace Green Room Sash
Install New Marquee & Entrance
Paint Base Tier Windows

*Air Conditioning and Accompanying Corridor Renovations*
Air Conditioning—Hotel Guest Rooms (Not Including Refrigeration)
Improvements to 2nd Floor Corridor and Guest Room Corridors
Emergency Lighting
Air Conditioning—Georgian Room

*Renovation of Main Lobby*
Refurbish Lobby
Improve Front Office Arrangement
Provide Additional Rentable Space

*Complete Renovation of Guest Bathrooms (139) and Replacement of Risers*
Provide Additional Guest Rooms by Altering Present Arrangements

*Modernization of 190 Guest Rooms*
Replace Obsolete Furniture
Removal of Old Telephone Boxes, Panel Molding, Wiremold
Improve Connecting Door Arrangement

*Installation of Radio and Television in Guest Rooms*

*Improvements to Public Dining Rooms*
　　Ladies' Rest Room—Brandywine Room
　　Improvements to Green Room Lighting

*Improvements to Private Function Rooms*
　　Convert West End Dishwashing Area to Ballroom Pantry
　　Renovate Rest Rooms, Ballroom, and Foyer
　　Renovate Du Barry Room Pantry

*Improvements to Food Preparation Area*
　　Experimental Kitchen
　　Install Additional Dishwashing Capacity
　　Renovate Green Room Pantry
　　Revamp Pot Washing Area
　　Completely Replace Obsolete Equipment with Stainless Steel

*Modernization of Commercial Offices*
　　Convert Store #22, Ground Floor, to Rentable Office Space
　　Alterations to Store #14

*Modernization of Elevators*
　　Replace Obsolete Service Elevators and Install Operatorless Controls for
　　All Elevators

*Additional Office Space and Hotel Guest Rooms*
　　Additions to the 12th and 13th Floors

TOTAL ESTIMATED COST: $5,000,000 Over a Three-Year Period

# Appendix H

*Comments from the Community*

The Hotel du Pont is an integral part of the community. We are pleased to set forth personal comments by a number of leading citizens of Delaware.

*The Rt. Rev. Arthur R. McKinstry,* 5th Episcopal bishop of Delaware and author of *All I Have Seen . . . The McKinstry Memoirs:*
"The Hotel du Pont has had more impact on the lives of the citizens of Delaware than any other institution."

*The Honorable J. Caleb Boggs,* governor, representative, senator of the State of Delaware:
"Hospitality, dignity, and excellence mark the Hotel du Pont's accommodations for all purposes and seasons. It is the place to meet. That is why we Delawareans are so proud of it."

*Lee Reese,* retired chairman of the News-Journal Co. and author of *The Horse on Rodney Square:*
"The still magnificent Hotel du Pont!"

*Charles A. Robinson,* retired chairman of the board of Delaware Trust Co.:
"The Hotel du Pont is one of the finest and most beautiful hotels in the world!"

*Clarence A. Fulmer,* educator and civic leader:
"I have been a patron of the Hotel du Pont for over 50 years. I have eaten over 2,000 meals there. The food preparation, service, and surroundings are excellent. All the rooms are elegant, and I consider the Gold Ballroom the most beautiful room in America. I have been in many of America's finest hotels, but our hotel, the Hotel du Pont, is *the* American hotel."

*Mrs. Thomas Herlihy, Jr.,* recipient in 1957 of the Marvel Cup, awarded annually to a citizen of Delaware for outstanding service to the community:
"A place of delightful memories during my teenage years. As time passes one learns to fully appreciate the quality and environment the Hotel du Pont provides. The friendly staff, the collection of art, and the decorative rooms combine to make family and friends' visits to the Hotel a memorable experience."

# Appendix I

*Comments from Travel Editors and Critics*

*Joseph A. Zebrowski, Jr., Fortune,* April 23, 1979:
"In the heart of Wilmington, Delaware, rests the Hotel du Pont, a grande dame asset of E. I. du Pont de Nemours & Co., Inc. Think of it, a hotel reflecting the corporate image of solidity, size, and efficiency."

*Robert Schwabach,* Philadelphia *Inquirer,* March 4, 1973:
"Wilmington's famous Hotel du Pont is a throwback to days when people did things right and ignored the cost."

*Andrew D. Wolfe,* Brighton-Pittsford (NY) *Post,* June 30, 1977:
"Imagine Paris without the Ritz, the George V, or the Crillon hotels, or New York without the St. Regis, the Plaza, or the Waldorf, but say one doesn't expect to find notable hotels in smaller metropolitan areas. Wrong—consider the Hotel du Pont, Wilmington, Delaware. Says a leading hotel and restaurant guide, 'This is one of the great hotels of the U.S.' Yes, the Du Pont is one of the great hotels of the country and it is a civic asset of exceptional dimension."

# Appendix J

*Comments from the Public Affairs Department of the
Du Pont Company*

*Robert P. McCuen,* director, Public Affairs Department:
"It's a convenience to have a fine hotel with complete facilities, including a superb kitchen, as an integral part of our
headquarters complex. But to anyone who is concerned with
public perceptions of Du Pont, as I am, the Hotel is more
than a convenience; it's an unexcelled communication device that speaks eloquently and persuasively about the character of the company. The Hotel says clearly that the organization of which it is a part is modern and efficient,
committed to high standards, yet warm and devoted to human values. I know that it does because people in this country and abroad go out of their way to tell me so.

"Du Pont's reputation is made of many things. The Hotel
is one of them, and I think that over the years it has been
one of the company's major public relations resources, thanks
to the quality of its services and the professionalism of its
staff."

*Thomas W. Stephenson,* retired director, Public Affairs Department:

"The Du Pont Company's reputation is derived from the character and competence of every unit within the organization. The company's good name is the accumulation of the integrity and performance of all its employees. For over 65 years the quality and service of the Hotel du Pont have contributed substantively and distinctively to the public's opinion of the Du Pont organization.

"The company prides itself on not undertaking anything it cannot do well. Expressed another way, once Du Pont decides to do something, nothing is spared and no detail is overlooked to do it as near perfectly as possible. The Hotel du Pont falls right into this tradition. Especially during the last 15 years when most major hotels have become sterile, routine, and impersonal, the Hotel du Pont has maintained warmth, class, and excellence."

*Harold Brayman,* retired director, Public Affairs Department, and author of *The President Speaks Off the Record:*

"From the time of its opening in 1913, the Du Pont Hotel, although relatively small, has ranked with the best commercial hotels in the country. It has been a great asset to the city of Wilmington in the services that it has provided to the people of New Castle County. It has been a convenient and suitable place for meetings of the boards of many local civic and charitable organizations, and almost never, in the 38 years I have known it, have I encountered a surly or unpleasant employee. It has always sought to give the best possible service to its customers at prices which, though they might seem high to some people, have been substantially below those of hotels of similar quality in New York, Philadelphia, and Washington. Without it, New Castle County would have been a less desirable place to live."